Spectacular Stinking Ro
Magazine Book

Pip Wilson is team leader of the Kingdom community called Romford YMCA. He is a Youth Worker by profession with years of experience in inner city, hostels and family centres. He is a trainer and gamester, well known for fast moving, totally hysterical, creative, anarchic, Rolling Magazine programmes featuring fun and development beyond frontiers.

He is also a Christian, writes regularly in the *Church of England Newspaper* and is author of *Gutter Feelings* and *Games Without Frontiers* (Marshall Pickering) and the Rolling Magazine Video (Greenbelt).

Ian Long is a radical Christian groovy Graphic Artist who overdoses on Communication Methods with a view to disturbing the comfortable and comforting the disturbed.

Other books by the author:

Gutter Feelings (Marshall Pickering)
Games Without Frontiers (Marshall Pickering)

Also by the same author:

Pip Wilson's Rolling Magazine Video (available from Greenbelt Festivals)

PIP WILSON'S SPECTACULAR STINKING ROLLING MAGAZINE BOOK

MarshallPickering
An Imprint of HarperCollins*Publishers*

First published in Great Britain in 1991 by
Marshall Pickering

Marshall Pickering is an imprint of
HarperCollinsReligious
Part of HarperCollins*Publishers*
77–85 Fulham Palace Road, London W6 8JB

Phototypeset by Intype, London
Printed and bound in Great Britain by
Hartnolls Ltd., Bodmin, Cornwall

A catalogue record for this book is
available from the British Library

Acknowledgements

Family for creating 'home base' and a special magazine lifestyle
Gill Holmes for translating my scrawl into English and the best
  of support.
R. M. Crew for the graft and sheer fun in delivering the best
  of communication.
Ian Long for bringing paper into life.
Greenbelt Board for inspiration and Rock 'n' Roll faith.
Christine Whitell for patience and endurance.
Jenny Orpwood for friendship and advice.
Howard Searle for linear lines in which sorrow and love flow
  mingled down.

And my many colleagues and friends who contribute to my
life and path – keeping me on the concrete way as we try to
demonstrate the Kingdom on Earth as it is in Heaven

Contents

Quarter Pages

Bits and Pieces

Group Games

End Games

Designing Your Own Games

SECTION THREE
The Rolling Magazine Video

Appendices

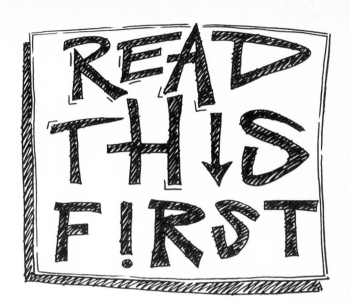

Watching Human People Grow

Youth Workers and people workers around the world are always looking for new ideas which they can keep 'on tap' or 'on shelf' to use appropriately.

Why?

Because we are into seeing human people grow. Because we desire to see humans open up like flowers do to the sun.

Everything I know to be good and have tried and unperfected, I have squeezed into this book. It is a collection of tools, ideas, ice breakers, stories, games and miscellaneous resources for youth workers, teachers, group workers, church workers, organisers of parties, camps, houseparties, training conferences and weekends. There is basic fun stuff plus loads of communication tools to take groups of beautiful humans into even more beautiful experiences.

As a youth worker for years, years and years and a Christian for most of that time I have collected, designed, tried and tested all sorts of activities, not just for fun – even though most are – but because I live to see God's number one creation – human creation – become more whole.

Whole being . . .

Growing in awareness of themselves
Growing in awareness of others around them
Growing in awareness of God and his aliveness
Growing in awareness of the world in which we live
Growing in skills to enable us to effect change in these areas.

I know that awareness raising is needed but I am also aware that skills need to be learned to enable the Kingdom of God to be established on earth as it is in heaven.

This book is interactive inviting you to participate. You don't have to read it all – start anywhere you like and follow your own journey.

Pick it up and explore – today, tomorrow, in five years' time. You will always find something fresh and practical.

Games for People with Disabilities

Jenny Orpwood, who is experienced in sports for disabled people, offers these guidelines for using games in a group of people of mixed abilities and disabilities.

Included with each game in this book is a guide as to whether or not a game is suitable for a person with a physical disability; a person who is deaf or has a hearing loss; and people who are blind or have a visual disability. The guide is only a rough indicator and should not necessarily be adhered to. As each person varies and is individual, so is disability, whether physical, perceptual or intellectual. It is, therefore, necessary to be sensitive to a person's abilities, rather than concentrating on disabilities.

PHYSICAL DISABILITY

An individual with a physical disability may be in a wheelchair, may walk on crutches or with aids, may walk unaided, or may have a disability that affects their arms. The disability may effect the whole body. This may mean an individual is unable to speak clearly, and may have poor mouth and throat control. Be wary of this in games involving holding things in the mouth. Limbs may be paralysed and have no feeling. Injury may occur without an individual knowing. This doesn't mean that she/he can't take part, but that a participant needs to know what is expected in the game and, therefore, know the risks involved.

It may be difficult for some people to dress and undress – be sensitive to this in games where it's required. ASK if help is required and what help is required. Some people with physical disability have learning problems – be sensitive in games requiring reading etc.

VISUAL DISABILITY

Very few people are totally blind. However, the degree to which some one can see will vary greatly. It may be useful, for example, to have materials such as the poems and blob pictures enlarged, which will aid many. Again, ask what help is required.

If lots of games are being played, ensure that not all of them involve just 'seeing' what's happening for the audience. It may be possible to 'see' people running backwards and forwards but not 'see' a face being made up. A good facilitator, giving a running commentary, will add to the atmosphere for everyone. Be sensitive when using reading or spelling games.

HEARING DISABILITIES

Again the degree of hearing loss will vary greatly. Those people who have extreme hearing loss may have poor speech also. Make sure that a person who is deaf is in the best position for seeing the person talking.

In discussion groups ask individuals to indicate when they are about to speak, and check that the lighting is good and that people don't cover their mouths, chew gum etc. whilst speaking. There's no need to shout, but speak clearly and at a moderate rate. Speaking very slowly distorts the mouth shape of the word. Writing things down may help. Many people who are deaf 'sign' – perhaps the group or leader could go on a course if appropriate. Again ask what's best for that person.

For people with a mental handicap it is difficult to give guidelines. Those given above for physical or perceptual handicaps may apply especially if an individual has a multiple disability. Remember to be sensitive when using word games – games which give the lead (like 'follow my leader') may be appropriate.

The most important point is to ensure that when a game is meant to include every one, it does so.

I've often been in a group in which the initial activity excludes someone with a disability. If a game is played to build the feeling of 'group' – make sure it does.

Don't be frightened of adapting games to suit the abilities of all people whether disabled or not.

GUIDES TO GAMES

👁	those with a visual disability
♿	those with a physical disability
👂	those with a hearing disability
√	most likely appropriate
X	most likely not appropriate
?	will suit some people

These should not be considered as absolute guidelines as every person is different even if they have the same impairment. If only visual or audible clues are given it may be necessary to consider using both for blind or deaf participants. For some disabled participants the eating games may be difficult. Remember some deaf people are unable to talk. Games which involve a lot of talking or discussion will be O.K. if members of the group are able to sign or there is an interpreter.

What is the Rolling Magazine all About?

The Rolling Magazine started because of a need at the Greenbelt Christian Arts Festival. The organisers wanted to see something happen between, on the one hand, the music programme with bands and the main stage, and on the other hand 'talk' seminars. Seminars are the equivalent of 'heavy' newspapers whilst the bands are a musical common ground for young adults. There was little in the middle which would fit the bill as a 'tabloidy' sort of communication. So that's how we started, thanks to Greenbelt wanting to meet the needs of young people.

Basically the target audience is teenagers, right up into their twenties. We get loads of teenagers into the Rolling Magazine Marquee with the idea of creating some sort of 'experience' with them – based on music. The music is loud – about 12,000 watts of contemporary music creates the backdrop into which drops a fast moving programme like stardust. All sorts of things happen. The principle is that if there is anything which is boring, it's actually over and finished with before people realise it's boring because you're on to the next quick action packed item in the programme. Basically the idea is instead of young people being preached at, talked at and so on, it is an experience of good news, an **experience** of the Gospel.

My input as leader of the team is key, but there is true participation as everybody present gets involved – up to a thousand young people at Greenbelt.

The Adaptable Rolling Magazine type of event can be adapted and used in many different contexts. Its basic need is a big enough crowd to create some group experiences. It can't be done in a front room, it can't be done in an 'after eight meeting' where there are only twenty people. It really needs more than that and a context where music can rock the place with vibes. Rolling Magazines can be experienced at houseparties, at camps and festivals, at carnivals, at any place where a number of people get together and as long as people are valued and affirmed.

People who receive this input will come together and hold hands and do groovy things like joining circles. Doesn't it sound boring on paper? You can get people talking to one another even though they've never met one another before. Really it's a structured experience. An experience is structured in the Rolling Magazine, facilitated by myself. Young people are encouraged to talk about certain things in a climate of trust. In real life, young people – and adults too – often stay at a certain level of communication (level one, if you know my themes and practice!). My objective is to take people into a depth of communication that is a beautiful experience.

Forget the Pip. The Rolling Magazine doesn't have to be Pip Wilson. It doesn't have to be Greenbelt. It doesn't have to be a big occasion if the principles are taken and applied. And the principles are that it's got to be fast moving and magazine, bitty, not something which is boring and of one style, but of several styles, several elements.

The base line is that people are valued, built up, affirmed and beautiful human persons. Humans are repeatedly affirmed – verbally and non-verbally – and this is expressed in every way.

Secondly, there's a music base which is contemporary pop, loud, with vibrancy. If you turn up the sound level, I find young people feel beautifully excited and relaxed and want to boogie and that boogie can effect them all the way through their lives – rock 'n' roll touches the inside as well as the outside of human lives.

One further element in the Rolling Magazine is that it's not just fun, though there has to be a massive percentage of real fun things, relaxing things. There is also a significant element which is developmental. You start where young people are at, but then you go along a road. An experiential exercise! So the Rolling Magazine gives lots of experiences as it takes young people along the road of self-discovery. Perhaps they're not allowed to be themselves. They discover a beautiful human person who is trying to get out! That takes a certain length of time, but eventually young people start to relax and to open up.

It seems to me everybody I know is like the bud of a beautiful flower. During the process of the Rolling Magazine that bud begins to open up like a flower to the sun. That is what we are meant to be – beautiful. What's inside is beautiful, trapped very often, and the Rolling Magazine objective is to get people to open up, speak to people alongside them, speak with people they've never ever met before. Often as facilitator I'll ask people, 'How many people are with somebody they've never met before?' and you'll see a group of ten kids holding hands or hugging one another. They have never ever met before, and yet, because they've entered into this climate of trust, they actually begin to trust one another and open up verbally, emotionally, to touch each other, to love the participation.

THE GAMES

There are all sorts of games. A number of the games are totally, totally crazy. For instance, we use materials such as eggs, flour, grapes, bananas and all sorts of sloppy stuff. They are slotted in throughout the programme alongside other games. For instance, a game may involve everybody in the tent talking to one another, with everybody holding hands with one another or hugging one another. Sometimes it's getting people to volunteer – I never push people to volunteer, and I never ever drag anybody up on stage.

Sometimes, for instance, I use a messy game called Grape Tread. The three participants have bowls with grapes in and they tread the grapes into wine. Then the wine is sieved into a glass and each participant has his or her own glass of grape juice. Then a 'count down' is given before the participants drink the fruit juice, to the glee of the audience.

As an added attraction to the game, and for audience impact, as the countdown is called, 5–4–3–2, I shout 'stop' and 'swop' and the participants swop the glasses of fruit juice and drink someone else's juice! It is drunk very willingly but obviously with all sorts of expressions on their faces.

Maybe it sounds quite a horrific game to play – but the audience love it. Even the participants love it because it is different from other activities and they can be proud of their achievement. If you've got a thousand young people in a big tent you can't play the games where people have got a little toothpick and a polo mint on the end! Passing a polo may be okay for people to play at a party with a small number of people. In a large auditorium you need lots of visual impact.

The games we play are totally non-competitive. There's never an emphasis on someone winning. The point is that we've had a good laugh and there's a certain outcome – we all can win.

We play interactive games which involve total participation. Young people may be asked to turn to one another and say, for instance, whether they would rather be the Prime Minister or his bodyguard. They have to decide instantly which one they want to be. Another is a choice between seeing the latest film or going for a walk in the countryside. Would you rather eat at a Chinese restaurant or an Indian restaurant?

The idea is to get people to disclose their own choice and then get a bit deeper. Describe what colour you are – not skin colour, but what colour do you think would describe your character, your personality? Young people will say they feel like a red person, or an orange person or a green person, and then I'll go on and say: "Okay, next question, what colour is God?" This facilitates young people saying what colour they feel God is. So in a very relaxed way a mass of people are talking about God, but not talking about him in religious terms, they're talking about how they *feel* about God.

One thing about God talk: I've never yet met a person in my life who has never prayed. There is a spirituality in every single person. Tap that spirituality which is often deep down in a person, and whoosh – out comes something which that person *believes* and *feels*!

This is stimulated by that whole process of self-disclosure. Often people don't know what they believe until they're disclosing to someone else. Self-disclosure helps to build people up, because they've shared something of themselves.

Paul Tournier puts it well:

We become fully conscious only of what we are able to express to someone else. We may already have had a certain inner intuition about it, but it must remain vague so long as it is unformulated.

(from *The Meaning of Persons*) – I love the title!

Few of us have experienced that very special relationship of being able to be totally open with another . . .

Oh the comfort, the inexpressible comfort, of feeling safe with a person, having neither to weigh thoughts nor measure words, but to pour them all out, just as it is, chaff and grain together, knowing that a faithful friend will take and sift them, keeping what is worth keeping, and then, with the breath of kindness, blowing the rest away.

Mary Ann Evans (George Eliot)

Therein rumbles a Rolling Magazine objective – Interaction at its best!

ROLLING MAGAZINE CONCEPTS – EH?

Obviously, The Rolling Magazine has certain targets and objectives. Its programme is not unthought out, even though it may be a total manic mess of quick firing happenings and experiences. There is a theology and a philosophy behind it all. One of the processes I try to take people through is to open up and to experience real communication.

I share something which I call the Five Levels of Communication and which has a "take-away" menu. Humans actually go home at the end of a Rolling Magazine communicating on Level 5. They talk to each other saying, "I'd like to talk in Level 5 with you." Take a look at the graphic on page 26.

Level 1 is when people talk in clichés. In normal life people talk about the weather, and that is very basic communication. Everybody does it, but let's face it, it's pretty boring!

Level 2 is when people talk about the facts – the football match, what has been on the TV soaps EastEnders or Neighbours. They merely regurgitate the facts of what they've seen.

Level 3 is when people start giving a little bit of themselves away through self-disclosure. That's when people give opinions – opinions about the football, opinions about the TV soaps.

Level 4 is when communication really starts to happen. Humans start to communicate about their feelings. They start to say, "I feel upset when such a thing happens," "I feel excited when such a thing happens," – and that is beautiful.

Level 5 is an extension of Level 4 feelings. Level 5 is total complete openness where people are in such a trusting climate

Level: 5

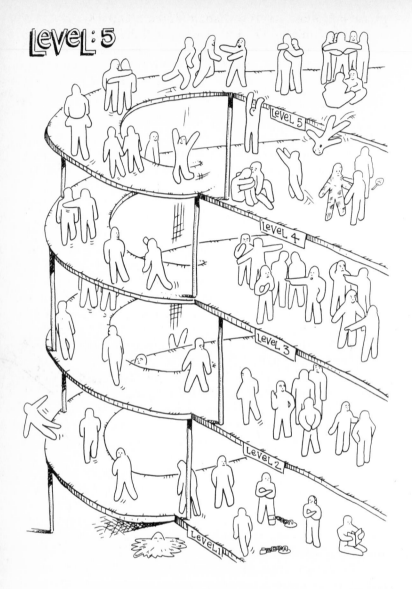

that they can communicate anything with total openness to someone whom they trust.

Obviously in the mayhem of a Rolling Magazine that is quite an objective – just to get all participants, including myself, to go through those levels of communication. Often we can only really communicate when we share the things which hurt us, feelings we suppress and push down. Let that out – and it becomes an experience of beautiful liberation. Of course the Christian Gospel is about liberation, about people experiencing freedom, and that is part of the Rolling Magazine.

THE PALM PERSON

A Palm Person can say "You are a beautiful human person" to the mirror. In the Rolling Magazine I introduce the Palm Person concept to help people see if they are one, or even whether they wish to become one!

A Palm Person is an open person, a warm person who communicates verbally and with non-verbal communication, symbolised by the exposed palms of the hands. Do you know that 80 per cent of communication is non-verbal? When God wanted to love the world he sent a human person – God incarnate.

The opposite to a Palm Person is the pointed finger communicator. That is someone who is usually telling you you "ought" to do this, or you "should" do that. Pointed finger person is sharp, aggressive, oppressive, authoritarian, and not a beautiful human communicator, it seems to me.

A Palm Person is about affirmation, not about the possession of another human, not defensive, not wanting to attack and compete. A Palm Person matches words and body to say: I am open, you are valuable. In the Rolling Magazine we encourage, practise and demonstrate the whole concept of being a Palm Person.

People like to think they have no strong feelings – especially against another Christian. It is really interesting to read in the Bible that right in the centre of the groups surrounding Jesus – there is conflict. I believe that conflict is part of life. Aggression is God-given, he has made us with an aggressive nature which has helped us to survive.

"Where there is no conflict there is no life," I often say. In fact, where there is no conflict you are dead! Whether we are at home or at work, our individual needs, values and views constantly and invariably differ from those of other humans. Some conflicts are relatively minor, easy to handle, or capable of being overlooked. Others are of greater magnitude and they require a strategy for resolving them.

Being a Christian means owning, that is, admitting, our life as it stands. But it also means living a life of growing into wholeness. This owning thing is very important to me, so let me spell it out: Owning is taking on board everything from our history. To 'own' is the opposite of avoidance. It is to experience freedom by being totally honest with ourselves. These concepts are all processed through the games in the Rolling Magazine. Like Stardust!

I don't know about you but I have met so many knotted up Christians and the ones who seem to be in the worst pain are the ones who don't own their problems. They don't own their feelings, they don't own their inferiority, they don't even own their arguments. They don't admit they have arguments with friends, and they certainly don't admit arguing with God. Some Christians have massive vulnerabilities and problems. We find that accepting and owning who we are actually helps us to live a liberated Kingdom life.

As we look back at the Bible we see similarities with the highly competitive world we live in.

The trouble is that Christians (and non-Christians, too) don't generally admit they're fighting for greatness. But there is a great sense of competitiveness rather than co-operation and interdependence. Jesus knew his disciples, and he owned the situation. He realised they wanted to be greater than the others, but he then said, "That shall not be the way among you," and he points us to the Palm Person Kingdom way. By owning our own life we become a Palm Person.

In the Rolling Magazine we acknowledge the two major drives within us. Psychologists say the two main drives are sex and power. A Palm Person acknowledges these drives but deals with them positively. Sex is beautiful, God made the drive, but yet just think of how horribly it can go wrong. Think of the rapes and other sexual assaults. In the midst of fun games, **real issues** are touched in the Rolling Magazine.

The power drive, if it's not used 'the Jesus way', is equally disgusting, equally obscene. Misuse of power is equal to incest because it oppresses little ones. The drives within us can be used very positively but they are not to be misused.

So a Palm Person is warm, open, a listener, has healing eyes that shine, knows pain that shows through transparency, and yet reflects in his or her body the Prince of Shalom. It seems to me that to become a Palm Person we first of all need to experience loving, and that is experienced in the Rolling Magazine.

Experience, know, feel God's love – that is an objective in the Rolling Magazine. That involves owning self, just recognising who you are. Own self, accept self, just love that person whom God loves (that's you). Just love that person whom Jesus died for (that's you). It seems to me this is the essential beginning of being a Palm Person.

From a position of security of being loved and feeling valued, we can then offer the same for people around us. The hope is that individuals and groups can take these essentials away with them when they leave the Rolling Magazine experience.

Another challenge is to raise awareness of vulnerability in oneself and in others. Be able to be a community maker, not a community breaker.

What about the takers in life? It makes me sad when we are hard on the takers. I admit there are so many around who don't give, they just take. It makes me wonder what pain they must be in. Here is a question: "What do *you* think about when you have toothache?"

In the Rolling Magazine some practical tips are given on becoming a Palm Person. One, never use a pointed finger. Two, always open palms in communication. Three, never say I "should" or you "should", seek alternative words. All these concepts come alive when experienced in a Rolling Magazine programme. There is more about this on page 159.

GUESTS

Everybody who is around is up for grabs in the Rolling Magazine. For instance, at the Greenbelt Festival we will invite in the celebrities – singers, songwriters, Martyn Joseph, Ricky Ross, whoever is aroun' we'll get them in to use their talents. The Rolling Magazine keeps on rolling, however, and they don't do their normal 'set' of half an hour. They come in and perform one number and then they're off – because we are off onto the next bubbly activity.

One of the challenges we love to create is to bring artistes down off their ten feet high stage to the reality of a stage which is eighteen inches high! Instead of their being Superstars, they actually become humans by expressing feelings. In a non-threatening way I'll ask the well known people about their own feelings, about their vulnerabilities, which I think the ordinary punters in the audience will identify with. That pop person becomes a real person as feelings and vulnerability are disclosed. The tough times of life are shared by us all – it's not all sweet and honey! So that's what we want to do. Get people to perform, but also get people to open up and become human. Fully alive humans – the objective of the Rolling Magazine.

Amongst our own crew we have artistes, too! One is a real artist who paints the banners and the artwork for us, Ian Long. He also makes vivid points via his artistic talent. He brings out sexuality or racial issues or some other issue which is current with impact art.

We also have Howard Searle, our poet. Howard communicates dramatically with humorous poems which are also very powerful and radically relevant to the day.

How's this for a poem.

Kissing

When Adam and Eve first got together
How did they know about kissing each other?
If you think about it, it's all rather strange really,
I suppose you could say, it's just like spitting at someone,
Though different accuracy and intensity is needed!
And one is a little more enjoyable than the other sometimes!
Just imagine it – coming home to the wife and kids
'Hello love' (spit spit) 'Hello kids' (flob flob).
Perhaps they first tried twiddling with each other's fingers
Which was all right and then messing with each other's hair
Which was boring after a while
And then finally rubbing their noses together
Until his slipped on hers and it happened.
The first ever kiss.
It just stuck after that.
If Adam had immediately afterwards started selling 'The
    Kiss'at a pound a time
He'd be a millionaire by now
And I'd be totally bankrupt!

Howard Searle

And here's one with a different objective.

Let's pretend

Let's pretend, let's pretend we're friends without having to
go to any trouble like getting to know each other.

Let's pretend, let's pretend we're friends, that we shared
our experience when we've only really been drinking
together.

Let's pretend, let's pretend we're close, though we only
want to joke or laugh, never listen or cry.

Let's pretend, let's pretend we're friends, that we can take
it automatically without ever having to give or try.

Let's pretend we're friends.

THE ROLLING MAGAZINE CREW

The crew is approximately twenty people. There's our DJ Dave
Harris, who has records, cassettes and CD machine plus the
video equipment to produce all the visuals and all the sounds.
We have also our stage manager, Friendboy, who keeps the
whole show co-ordinated. The crew, amongst many other
activities, facilitate the games materials so that they're ready to
use instantly. *Someone*'s got to get ready the Baked-Bean Trifle,
and the porridge dyed with multi-colour ugliness. We have
oranges, bananas and lemons, and miscellaneous materials
which facilitate our 'no programme' programme of heavenly
chaos.

In the Rolling Magazine we have a repertoire but we never
have a set programme. The Crew also participate on the stage,
sometimes by just dancing, or they go right out into the audience and get involved in the games and help people relax and
rock and roll.

LEADERSHIP

The leader of this type of event needs to be someone who is
sensitive to group dynamics. Just to be able to see a group of
young people and to be aware of them is important. For
instance, if there's anyone who is disabled, physically or men-
tally, it's bad news to play a game which is likely to leave
anyone out. You just have to adjust whatever game it is. Some

people in wheelchairs can play a game where participants are holding hands, but obviously they can't play a game where everyone is physically rolling over one another on the floor! So you've got to be stinking sensitive to that.

You've also got to be secure in who you are yourself. Your main concern is reading the audience and responding to their needs. Don't "fall out" with the audience. It's bad news to shout at them and "tell them off" in any way. Encourage them to participate. Leaders need to be people who can value themselves so they can, in turn, value other people. Often people who put other people down have very low self-esteem, so a Rolling Magazine leader needs to be someone who can aim to love unconditionally.

If you find that difficult, remember: "There are no difficult people, there is only difficult behaviour."

OBJECTIVES

The objectives of a Rolling Magazine are to get people to relax, to get involved and to experience something which is very, very positive for their lives. It is life-giving, life-building and builds fully-aliveness! Rolling Magazine participating humans need to take things away with them at the end of the experience.

It seems to me that the learning process in life is often not through books, through lectures and through seminars. The most powerful influence in our lives often is our culture. All our cultural norms, which we carry around every day in something much closer than a backpack, have been learned over a process of years – not by somebody preaching at us but by soaking them in like sponges! We soak up values, morals, attitudes, spirituality and lots of things which are important to us.

The Rolling Magazine experience is about soaking up beautiful things. Throughout a Rolling Magazine evening or weekend, sprinklings of stardust soak into the sponge of our life and afterwards we can take these things away because they've been experienced. Part of that is Level 5 communication – being able to talk about feelings, being able to enjoy yourself, being able to approach a stranger and say something which is meaningful and affirming.

In the Rolling Magazine you don't need to step back in life and be a wallflower. New skills can be learned – the experience of love, the sharing of love. My main concern isn't about the success of the Rolling Magazine as an event, it is to find methods which help to develop young people individually, as groups, as little church fellowships. I want activities which will actually get people to open up and to grow.

One of the basic principles of the Christian faith is that *everybody is loved and valued by God*, unconditionally, totally, 100 per cent. That is a basic principle, and a firm foundation to build on. We need to go on, to grow into more beautiful humans, to reach the stature of Christ, as it says in the Bible – so everyone needs to grow.

Obviously people grow at different paces so one of the objectives of the Rolling Magazine is to provide a growth experience which allows people, in a relaxed way, to push out their own boundaries, however limited or wide they are. It seems to me that we all stay within our boundaries; they are like comfort zones in which we operate, talk and meet people. An objective of the Rolling Magazine is to take people outside those to where growth occurs. You only grow when you take risks, it seems to me. The Rolling Magazine creates opportunities where people can take risks in a climate of trust.

To laugh is to risk appearing the fool.
To weep is to risk appearing sentimental.
To reach out is to risk involvement.
To expose feelings is to risk exposing your true self.
To place your ideas and dreams before the crowd is to risk
    their love.
To love is to risk not being loved in return.
To live is to risk dying.
To hope is to risk despair.
To try is to risk failure.
But the greatest hazard in life is to risk nothing.
The one who risks nothing does nothing and has nothing –
    and finally is nothing.
S/He may avoid sufferings and sorrow,
But s/he simply cannot learn, feel, change, grow or love.
Chained by certitude, s/he is a slave; s/he has forfeited
    freedom.
Only one who risks is free!

Author Unknown

SHALOM

The concept of Shalom helps me to be who I am – and to do what I do. Shalom has been the most helpful Bible revelation in my life and I am eager to pass it on. Shalom is a Hebrew word which is translated 'peace' in our English Bibles. I sometimes say, "No Shalom for the wicked"!

Most commentators agree that the common usage of "peace" means the experience of internal well-being, whilst the word Shalom is much broader to encompass physical and general welfare too. It goes beyond the personal to positive relationships between individuals and among groups – fulness of joy in real relationships. "Shalom is the gift of God", said Bishop Stuart Blanch. It is dynamic, it encompasses society, it is harmony, dignity, freedom, justice – in fact it's true to say "The Shalom of God passes all understanding".

I used to think my job as a Christian was limited to telling others about Jesus and seeing conversions. Shalom theology shows me that God's aim is also seeing a homeless young person settle into a home, finding freedom from insecurity, learning life skills, developing, and many other growth areas so he can experience, feel, know and become a branch in a tree rather than a pebble in a box. Shalom is also about the Berlin Wall coming down, Mandela being free, racism removed from all nations including the only one which has a constitution enshrining racism.

Shalom also makes the Rolling Magazine rock 'n' roll instead of being a big lecture factory. It makes fun as well as making real issues live. It stretches every laughter muscle instead of just the "I am a sinner" glands. Shalom liberates, releases, sets us free. Shalom is one word to replace the two words of Rolling Magazine. God made Shalom through his son's death on the cross (Colossians 1.20).

KISSING FOR BEGINNERS

We do kissing, too. Sometimes I'll say to the Rolling Magazine crowds, "What have you been missing?" and everybody will shout, "We've been missing the kissing!"

Picture this. I'm interviewing people on the stage in the middle of a game. I could be saying, "Where are you from? What's your name?" All the audience are shouting out, "Hello

James! Hello Nicky! Hello Gloria!" and so on. Picture all that participation going on. Then if I find a couple who have a kissing relationship (i.e., for simple readers, they're actually going out with one another) I'll get their partner out of the audience and get them to swoon to each other and to demonstrate a kiss! The whole of the audience and the couple themselves love it.

Some people think you "Shouldn't do that at Christian events", but believe me, we all love the physical interaction called kissing. A kissing experience is just beautiful. It is claimed that every kiss shortens the lifespan by three minutes! The choice is yours!

Stop tooth decay by kissing! It is claimed that the extra saliva, which kissing promotes, washes food particles off the teeth, lowers acid levels, helps reduce plaque build-up, and saves bus fare on travel to your dentist!

In a Rolling Magazine we practise kissing – between consenting adults, of course!

I am being flippant here. "Kissing talk" is the term I use when approaching issues of sexuality or "touching" – in a nice friendly way. Let's be honest about kissing, about sexuality. It is so powerful and so relevant to us all, and yet it gets pushed into the margins of Christian teaching. It seems to me we mustn't allow sex to be oppressive. It needs to be integrated as part of "whole life", not separated and whispered about. "If God is Lord at all, he is Lord of all." Sex, however, is often pushed into a corner and cut off from the rest of life.

It needs to be integrated into our belief system, so that we *do* as we *believe* – rather than letting our behaviour decide what we believe. Our faith needs to be the guiding force for all our body functions and body parts. Our behaviour is highly visible to others and it needs to demonstrate what we believe. Communication needs to remain open, especially for such a powerful drive as the sexual one. It's so easy to take on board the "jousting" or competitive ideas about sex that come across in the media with its emphasis on the physical.

All this links in with relationships in general, not just marriage – we all need to be in human contact. Remember we need to be God with skin on! – this crops up later in this book. All of us need to be in open and honest communication with people around us, and that includes handling body contact well. Some of the saddest people I meet have confessed that they have not touched anyone for a long time. That doesn't include shaking hands, which is not touch, but ritual. But we need to watch ourselves when it comes to real touching.

It seems to me that touching can easily be misunderstood and it needs always to be matched with words. Aim for total crystal clear communication – not just touch! Any group of young adults – or older adults – need to give each other permission to discuss and decide how they conduct themselves. It is possible for this to include body contact done lovingly and sensitively without being contaminated by inappropriate sexual innuendo.

Our culture – every culture – has suffered from the fall of humankind. The inhibitions we carry are part of our fallenness – remember the Genesis story when Adam and Eve only realised they were naked after they had sinned. So as we proceed to establish God's Kingdom back into his world, we need to battle with the fallenness that inhibits our touching of fellow humans.

So touch people – as long as it doesn't oppress. It needs to be Good News. If it doesn't come naturally – think, talk and decide your pattern of Kingdom touching!

A Bible verse: "And as many as touched him were made perfectly whole" (Matthew 14.36).

A GOOD GAME

One game I play is to get the whole assembled crowd to "make love"! You might say, "What's this then?" (Worried frown on brow! Humans walking past get anxious, wondering what's going on in there!)

I simply get groups of ten people or so together and I get them to make with their bodies the word L-O-V-E (see page 213). Then while around the tent everybody is making L-O-V-E, I go round taking photographs of the best ones. It's a wonderful, fun, participation game enjoyed by anyone with any decent amount of energy. Once I remember a group, amongst a thousand or so young people "making love", who shaped with their bodies the three letters G-O-D.

Games Section

Introduction to All Games

There is a mass of games here, divided simply into six sections each with its own introduction. Please note that Book I, *Games without Frontiers* has many many games – a small number are repeated or developed here.

Games are childish?

If you have never led or participated in these sort of games – remember your own childhood and your own growth and participation in your own particular culture. I guess it included games with the other kids? Games are not childish, they are wonderful for adults and a freeing experience for all. Games are usually active, participating, relaxing, humourful and can also be a learning experience. Anyway – we all have a "child" inside us, and isn't it wonderful to let ourselves come out to play?

Hints and tips for you to use, ignore, or bits between these two extremes. Do have objectives for all you do. Even the most silly party game, or camp type messy game, needs to be led well by a person with clear objectives. If the aim is just to have fun, that is an objective, and "owning" this will help the facilitation of a game. See The Objectives Index. It will reveal all games suitable for your particular objective – for that particular group of humans who are special and unique.

Know your Context. It is important for anyone who facilitates a game or series of games, to discover as much information as possible about the following:

The Venue	Size of room (or tent, field, hall), carpeted, lighting, ceiling height, stage fixed/portable, and size.
The Atmosphere	The likely atmosphere – obviously influenced by their sex/age mix, expectations, social background, ethnic mix, one group – or

mixed groups, religious group, hostile, recent programme, and the expectations and attitudes of the organisers.

Equipment	Get it – know it – it is important.
Timescale	Know your start and finish boundaries. Setting up time is vital and often takes longer than you expect.
Process	Don't dive straight in with games of intensity. Ice Breaker followed by a lead into intensity, if that's your objective. Note 'five levels of communication' page. It applies to games too!
Facilitate a Climate of Trust	Encourage, value, thank and affirm in all you do. Be aware of your own feelings and those of others. You are there to meet their needs.
Humour	Laughter is a leveller. Relaxing to extreme. Being "fully alive" is being able to laugh a lot, it seems to me.
Liberation or Oppression?	Offer all you do freely but not as "shoulds" and "oughts". People will take and receive much more if they feel it's not being pressed upon them. I often say to the assembled humans . . . "Open your palms to receive all that happens. If it is useful to you – cup it in the palm of your hands and take it with you when you go. If you don't want it, it's no good to you – open your hand and let it slip through your fingers like sand running to the ground."
Straight from the Shoulder Quick Tips	Always have a First Aid Kit. Be aware of the isolated person. Be aware of disability of all and every kind. Value, encourage, affirm. Know, and go for, your objectives.

Ice Breakers

Ice Breakers are so called because they are games that are supposed to melt the ice, relax the atmosphere, at the start of a
particular gathering of humans. Two things can go wrong: (1)
Using an inappropriate game; (2) Inappropriate facilitation by
the leader.

Some people are hostile to games. They have had bad experiences or have extreme feelings of unease about mixing with
others. A good Ice Breaker is a 'structured experience' – structured by you, the facilitator or leader (whichever title you like
best!). A good introduction before the game will set a climate
of trust. A gentle lead into the game will, using the formulas
outlined in the Games Introduction above, prepare even the
most fearful heart.

Don't forget that there will be apprehension at the beginning
of a conference, training course, weekend, meeting, da de da.
Unless it is a small group who know each other very well, and
are extremely cohesive, the participants will be apprehensive.
There may be a number of masks worn. Shells of respectability
and sociability often hide real unease. Be aware of the inner
person, not just the the shell – *Love the inner person*.

Last point. You cannot play "Ice Breakers" all evening. In
themselves they are a preparation for something deeper and
more objective. The "Vote with your Feet" Ice Breakers which
follow are, however, good examples of a game which can be
played over a considerable period of time – But the early part
of the game can be "icebreaking", moving on to greater and
greater depth.

Ice Breaker: Vote With Your Feet

OBJECTIVE

To get a medium-to-large group to mix informally by getting them to "buzz talk" together on any relevant topic. These activities are useful at the start of a Rolling Magazine, or at the beginning of a conference or training course.

DETAILS

Get everyone standing. Ask people to walk to one or the other side of the room, depending on their choice of answer to questions. Simple example: "Would you choose to eat at an Indian restaurant or a Chinese restaurant?" They then walk to one side of the room or the other.

The choice they make often leaves people standing next to someone they don't know, or at least by a different person every time. At this point, give them a one-minute task to talk together about something – easy at first, becoming more deep and stretching (and fulfilling) as time goes on. See the list of suggested self-revelation topics.

Once icebreaking discussion has taken place move on to discussions relating to the purpose of the meeting/conference/course.

Don't drag it out!

NOTES

1. Explain your objective – so people don't think you are crazy!
2. Start simple – offer non threatening choices (as above, and there are more below).
3. Benefits are:

   i Informal method of mixing people, getting people to talk to strangers.

    ii Ice-breaking generally.

    iii Tuning into the agenda/activity to follow. You can select an appropriate subject.

4. Be aware. Feelings are running high at the start of an event/conference. Usually there is some apprehension. The easy approach of this game usually breaks this down.

5. Be sensitive. These activities do create feelings amongst participants. Be sensitive and affirmative, the idea is to break ice not create hostility.

6. Be careful not to isolate individuals. Questions like 'Born in this country' can be very good to use but the facilitator (you) needs to be sensitive. At all costs avoid dividing the group so that one person is on one side and the rest on another.

7. Usually there are significant differences in tastes, choices, attitudes, between young people and youth workers. These can be big . . .

    It is always a challenge for youth workers to find common ground with young people. It is good to be aware of cultural differences.

CHOICES: FACTS OR TASTES

Do you prefer:

Indian Restaurant	Chinese Restaurant
The Sun	*The Guardian*
Coronation Street	Neighbours
Liked School	Didn't Like It
Cinema	Theatre
Giver	Taker
Disco	Countryside
McDonalds	Pizza Hut
Steak	Hamburger
Football	Rugby

Are you:

Leader	Follower
Tortoise	Hare
Thinker	Doer
Reliable	Unreliable
Optimist	Pessimist
Went to church last Sunday	Didn't go to church last Sunday

Talker	Listener
Believe in God	Don't believe
Born in this town	Not born here
Born in this country	Born elsewhere

CHOICES: HUMOROUS

Would you rather be:

Mother Teresa	Dame Edna
Humpty Dumpty	King's man (or woman)
Batman	Robin
Prime Minister	Bodyguard

Do you:

Clean the toilet	Not
Eat pig	Not
Wear boxer shorts	Underpants

Have you:

Kissed today	Not yet

IDEAS TO TALK ABOUT: SELF-REVELATION

Favourite time of day
Favourite place in house
Favourite season
Favourite holiday
Favourite hobby
Favourite sport
Favourite Pop Star
Favourite author
Favourite TV Programme
Favourite Radio Programme
Favourite meal
Favourite car
Favourite flavour of crisps
Colour to describe Monday
Colour to describe own character
Colour to describe God
Significant person in your life as a child
What makes you sad?
In what way are you rich?
In what way poor?

If you could smash one thing . . .
If you could swop one body part . . .
Last phone call would be to . . .
Name a car like self
Name a car like God
Name a warm person in your life
What do you do with toenails when cut?
Which bit do you wash first in the bath?
Which piece of clothing do you take off first?

VARIATION FOR YOUTH WORKERS

1. Do Vote With Your Feet using the sample questions or your
   own ideas.
2. When ice is broken ask the group to choose one young
   person whom they work with or go to school or college with,
   and to talk about that person to someone they are standing
   with during the activity. (This helps the young person to
   come alive in the mind.)
3. Then get the individuals in the group to become the young
   person they have chosen. Now ask the same questions/
   choices as before and ask the youth workers to respond as
   they guess the young person would respond. This raises
   awareness. Experiential! Demonstrating the difference
   between worker and young person. Discuss.

Messy Games

Introduction to Messy Games

In the right location and context these games are "fun" in the extreme. Reading them you will immediately understand that they may be better played in an outdoor situation – generally speaking. Be careful *where*, *when* and *which* you use. The enclosed is not a list to run down using one after another. Any one of them would be ideal to end a fun session with. Others could be used mid-stream as could others in this book and my previous book *Games Without Frontiers* (Marshall Pickering, 1988). Essential for these games: Good attractive equipment, a good build up, very willing volunteers and a flexibility in operation.

Go for it and enjoy it too!

WARNINGS

1. Always have a *First Aid Kit* available.
2. Never press, force or embarrass a person to play a game.
   . Encouragement is the best.
3. Be aware of the odd one out.
4. Be aware of people who are disabled.
5. Don't play 'emotionally stirring' games unless you can give the experience and the time to work through the effects.

Babies

OBJECTIVE

Stunt game with impact and fun for participants and spectators

NUMBERS

3 couples with spectator participants

EQUIPMENT

3 baby bottles
3 bibs
3 baby bonnets
3 cans of coke (or similar canned drink)

DETAIL

Build the game up as a simple coke drinking competition. In reality it's a contest with the girls feeding the drink to the boy from baby bottles filled with coke.

Start the countdown from 10 to zero, then stop before zero. Then bring out the bonnets and bibs and dress the boys. Then do the countdown and the race is to finish the drink first.

| X | X | √ |

Egg Pit

OBJECTIVE

Extremely good fun for spectators and gamesters.

NUMBERS

3 people or more.

EQUIPMENT

3 eggs per person
Set of stilts

DETAILS

Start the "wind up" by saying it is a stilt race around the hall/tent/marquee (whatever your context). Start the count-down, then stop and bring on the eggs. Now place eggs under gamesters' armpits and chins. Then they race round the course on stilts.

NOTES

Make stilts with empty paint cans, with string or rope handles – or get more sophisticated ones.
   If you want to be really wicked, blindfold the contestants.

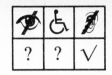

Umbrella Gunge Game

OBJECTIVE

An extremely messy stunt game for extremely messy fun.

NUMBERS

3 couples

EQUIPMENT

3 umbrellas (clear plastic ones from the local market stall)
3 jugs of water
3 jugs of powder paint (non-toxic)
3 tins of spaghetti hoops (family size)

DETAILS

Tape the umbrellas so they are fixed half open and unable to be closed or opened fully.

One from each couple holds the umbrella upturned and they get ready to race a prepared course around the location (you will get into trouble if it is indoors!) On "Go" the other partner pours the water into the umbrella and they both run – participants holding umbrellas down as they go.

On their return the losing couple has to lift umbrella over their heads and receive the deluge of water.

Before the next lap is run give them jugs of paint to put into the umbrellas. Run the race and the losers empty the contents over themselves in a leader-led hyped-up manner.

The last lap is run with the spaghetti hoops in the umbrellas. End this lap by asking knock-out questions (see samples). Ensure two out of three couples get messy. It's a challenge to get the winner to volunteer to upturn the umbrella.

SAMPLE QUESTIONS – See Appendices

Chucky Egg

OBJECTIVE

Messy fun – especially for the watching crowd.

NUMBERS

2 couples

EQUIPMENT

Egg chucky machine (to be well made, see suggestion below)
1 large mallet (best home made – very big!)
½ dozen tomatoes
½ dozen eggs
BIG Hats (made from cardboard with no top, see below)

DETAILS

Get two couples to volunteer, interview them to create personal involvement by the audience. One member from each couple goes into the audience with a hat on. Their partners use the machine to chuck a tomato – test run with the tomatoes. Basic idea is to catch the flying eggs/tomatoes in the hat. It is done in competition style, but the main aim is to make a mess on someone's head and provide spectator enjoyment.

Water Team Pass

OBJECTIVE

Good splashing fun for all.

NUMBERS

All in groups of about 10 people.

EQUIPMENT

1 plastic cup for everyone in the group
Water

DETAILS

Each group stands in a circle, all with cups in their mouths – held by the lip of the cup. One person has a cup filled with water, whilst holding it in the mouth. On "Go", the group sends water around the circle without hands, from cup to cup. Emphasis is on fun – not competition.

NOTES

Ideal on a hot summer's day by the pool, on a campsite. Even more fun when people are in normal clothing!

Shock Shower Bingo

OBJECTIVE

Fun spectator game.
Extremely messy game of chance with a view to suicidal volunteers and excited spectators.

NUMBERS

3 couples

EQUIPMENT

Shock Shower built up as follows:
    One cheap shower curtain unit from your local DIY.
    Support rail – screwed to an old door.
    Paddle pool – to receive and contain the mess!
3 large jugs – one-litre capacity ideal
3 litres red paint (non-toxic children's powder type from local art shop, or 3 litres custard (water based)
3 litres rice pudding (water based)
3 litres of confetti
3 Chairs

DETAILS

Prepare equipment well – with adequate helper back-up. Couples compete to decide order of entry into shower. First in gets the first deluge. Decide order of entry by, for example, a Balloon blow and burst race, or eating two cream crackers. The first couple get the rice pudding, the second get the custard. Final participants get the third deluge, the paint, plus a second helping of confetti.

SPECIAL NOTES

The build-up and fun element are as important as the stunning effect of the colourful gunge.

The old door provides a colourful visual aid if painted attractively.

This game is extremely messy and yet has a wonderful visual impact for a large crowd. Only attempt if there is a commitment from volunteers to take 'the worst'.

Present a prize to *all* participants – they deserve it!

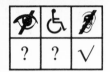

Welly Gunge

OBJECTIVE

Messy fun. Good for spectators and participants.

NUMBERS

3 couples

EQUIPMENT

3 pairs of large wellies – the largest available
3 jugs of water
3 jugs of custard
3 tins of spaghetti rings

DETAILS

One sockless bare-footed person from each couple wears the wellies. (Choose volunteers who don't have large calves as you need space down the side of the wellies for the gunge!)
On "Go" they have water poured into the wellies, then they race around the course. When they get back to "Go" the other items are deposited in the wellies.
The prize is offered to the best one to handstand up against their partner. Do this one at a time. For effect count down from 5 to zero – "Go"!
Just before the last one does the handstand you shout "Stop – Swop". The last couple swop roles – the wellies come off and go on the cleanfooted partner. The countdown and the handstand are the climax.
Prizes for all are recommended.

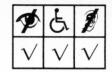

Custard Feed

OBJECTIVE

Really good visual fun.

NUMBERS

3 couples

EQUIPMENT

6 plastic aprons (exclude if context permits – it's more fun!)
6 coloured bowls or jugs
6 big plastic spoons – the bigger the better
6 litres of thick custard
6 blindfolds
6 chefs hats

DETAILS

The aim is to feed each other whilst blindfolded.
Set up all ready to go and . . . then bring in blindfolds
It's visual, and a good laugh.
It's supposed to be a race to eat the custard – but the real objective is the messy fun.

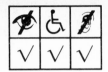

Marshmallow Stuff

OBJECTIVE

Good fun

NUMBERS

3 volunteers

EQUIPMENT

3 bags of marshmallows
3 blindfolds
3 chairs
(Can also be done with other items, e.g. mixed bags of fresh fruit.)

DETAILS

Have the 3 blindfolded and sit them on chairs with a packet of marshmallows each. Tell them that it's a competition and the winner is the one who can eat the most in 3 minutes. Arrange for 3 others to do the counting and someone to do the time-check. Give the signal to go and encourage loud shouts for each of the contestants. However, after about 15 seconds quietly take the blindfolds off two of them, telling them to go back to their places leaving just one person stuffing his or her face. As your audience are still shouting for all 3 (you keep pointing to the empty chairs) the unfortunate person left thinks the competition is still on. After about 2 minutes signal to the audience to stop as you remove the blindfold.

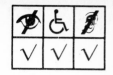

Banana Fizz

OBJECTIVE

Spectator fun

NUMBERS

3 volunteers

EQUIPMENT

3 cans of lemonade and 6 bananas

DETAILS

Set up a race to see which of the 3 volunteers can peel 2 bananas, eat them, and drink a can of lemonade the fastest. Watch their mouths foam up, give the winner a bunch of bananas and six-pack of lemonade.

NOTES

Shake cans of lemonade a little.

Vaseline Nose

OBJECTIVE

A fun race – good to watch too!

NUMBERS

The game may be played with individual competitors or with relays. Everyone present can play if materials permit, or two teams of 6 to 10.

EQUIPMENT

Loads of cottonwool balls
1 very large washing-up type bowl for cottonwool balls
2 buckets – colourful – why be boring?
Jar of vaseline

DETAILS

Each team has to carry cottonwool balls across a line and drop them into a bucket. The cottonwool balls may be carried only on the nose by volunteers smearing some Vaseline on their noses. On hands and knees, members poke their noses into cottonwool balls. When they get a ball to stick they crawl a couple of feet to the line and disengage the ball by blowing or head shaking.

SPECIAL NOTES

Variations on the game are immense. Adapt as you see fit.

Lemon Aid

OBJECTIVE

Fun race with cringe factor for all

NUMBERS

3 volunteers

EQUIPMENT

3 lemons
3 cups of water

DETAILS

Introduce it as a lemonade drinking competition. Say you've forgotten the lemonade. In reality it's a race to eat a raw lemon – peel and pips and all! I often get strong men to volunteer for this. Wind up the need to be strong, tough. Only reveal the race materials once they are plugged in to volunteering. Their mates will cajole them to doing the game – distasteful or not.

Jam Race

OBJECTIVE

Good fun for all

NUMBERS

All present in teams

EQUIPMENT

Jar of jam
Loads of cottonwool balls

DETAILS

Everyone puts jam on their nose and stands in line. The end one places a cottonwool ball on nose, and on "Go" the wool ball is passed down the line without hands. Dropped cottonwool balls mean a restart.

SPECIAL NOTES

Good fun camp type game

⌀	♿	🏃
?	?	√

Spooning

OBJECTIVE

Wet fun

NUMBERS

2 or 3 couples

EQUIPMENT

1 plastic cup for each couple
1 big spoon for each couple
1 bucket of water

DETAILS

One from each pair lays on his or her back with cup on forehead, close to a chair. On "Go" the other partner races back to the bucket of water – spoons some up, carries it back, stands on the chair, and empties the water into the cup. The aim is to fill the cup full inside 1 minute.

NOTES

A wet game! It can be played with a team of runners. All the team can have a go – fill a bucket!

Shoot It Out

OBJECTIVE

Wet fun game

NUMBERS

3 couples

EQUIPMENT

Paper plates, short candles, water pistols, ribbon, matches – for each participant.

DETAILS

Construct Candle Hats out of paper plates, ribbon and short candles. The candle is secured with candle wax on top of the upside-down plate. Ribbon is used to tie the hat on the head. The volunteers wearing the candle hats are given water pistols and placed 3–3½ metres apart. The candles are lit. On "Go" they dual to be the first to squirt out the other's lighted candle.

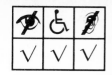

Blind Spoonfuls

OBJECTIVE

Fun

NUMBERS

3 volunteers

EQUIPMENT

6 large colourful bowls – kitchen type
3 spoons – big heavy kitchen type
Cottonwool balls
3 blindfolds

DETAILS

People are seated in front of a table facing the audience. The equipment is placed in front of them before they are blindfolded.
Each has two bowls, one full of cottonwool balls, one empty.
The objective is to fill the empty one using the spoon – only.
The spare hand must be placed on the head.
Just before "Go", blindfold the participants, then quickly remove the bowl with wool balls returning it empty.
On "Go" they race ahead – doing exactly nothing.

NOTES

Try leaving one with cottonwool balls, the other two with none.

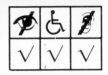

Eggstacle Race

OBJECTIVE

Cracking good fun – messy

NUMBERS

3 volunteers

EQUIPMENT

2 dozen eggs
Large packet of cornflakes
A blindfold for each participant

DETAILS

Show the participants two dozen eggs on the floor and explain that the objective is to walk from one end of the course to the other through the field of eggs, blindfolded.

When they are blindfolded, get some members to pick up the eggs quietly and cover the floor in cornflakes. Background noise may be needed to hide the sound of the operation.

Place an egg under the chin and under both armpits of each blindfolded volunteer.

On "Go" spin each person round 3 times to disorientate them, then point them in the right direction.

If adequate cornflakes have been used, each step will bring a crunching sound similar to stepping on eggshells.

At the end of the course, say the prize is a big hug – everyone hugs the 3, crushing the eggs under the armpits and chin. Then show them the cornflakes.

Fun Games

Introduction to Fun Games

When I look down this list I get excited. There are some incredible games – ideal for your Christmas party, birthday, club event, or mixed into a whole programme of 'events' similar to the Rolling Magazine.

Have Fun!

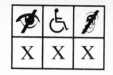

I'm All right, Jack

OBJECTIVE

Real good fun

NUMBERS

Ideally 10 to 15

EQUIPMENT

Pack of cards

DETAILS

Everyone sits in a circle around a table. One person has the pack of cards and slaps them down in the centre of the table one at a time, face upwards.

When the cards listed below come into view, the whole group follows the instructions (they're easy to learn).

Have a good try – learning the game is fun. Rotate the card dealer.

When familiar with the game – start again. The one who is slowest at doing the actions drops out until a winner is found. Remember the objective is fun – not winning!

THE ACTIONS

Any Jack: everyone shouts "I'm all right, Jack"
Any Queen: everyone stands and does a curtsey
Any King: everyone stands and salutes
Any Ace: everyone stands and moves to the next seat in the circle
Any Seven: everyone does all the above in the above order

| ? | ? | √ |

Slipped Disc

OBJECTIVE

Fun

NUMBERS

Groups of ideally 8 or 10

EQUIPMENT

One paper plate per group

DETAILS

Groups lie face down on the floor, in a circle, with heads to the centre. One person has a paper plate between shoulder blades. On "Go", the game is to transfer the paper plate from person to person around the circle without dropping the plate.

√	X	√

Lean On Me

OBJECTIVE

Experiencing trust and fun

NUMBERS

Any number above 2

EQUIPMENT

None

DETAILS

Everyone in twos standing back-to-back, touching.

Both gently lean on each other while at the same time stepping slightly away from each other. On the word "Go" the couples slowly bend legs to squat position and up again. Emphasize need for trust, discourage fooling about.

It's really good to see/experience a mass demonstration of this. Next try it in threes, fours, possibly fives. It's difficult beyond that number.

Suck Blow Game

OBJECTIVE

Participation fun party game

NUMBERS

All in groups of about 10

EQUIPMENT

One playing card for each group

DETAILS

Group stand in circle, boy/girl/boy, etc. One person holds the card flat to the mouth kissing it, then passes it to the next person by sucking it to hold, blowing to release. No hands!

NOTES

Good party game – it can be hysterical. Far better than pass the polo!

I'm Touched

OBJECTIVE

Group fun, ice breaker

NUMBERS

One group, or as many small groups as possible.

EQUIPMENT

None

DETAILS

Everyone gets into groups, or it can be done in a large crowd. The leader calls out "touch . . . (name a body part or object)" and everyone has fun touching their forefingers on the named items. People keep touching the item until next instruction is given.

Some examples:

| A watch | A nose | A shoe | Something red |
| A ring | A knee | A sock | Something blue |

NOTES

A good way to end the activity is to call attention to each person's fingerprint on the index finger. Have them look at it, feel it. Emphasise the uniqueness of that fingerprint, and the uniqueness of the person. Affirm and value. In a warm, sensitive manner, ask everyone present to press their unique fingerprint, their uniqueness, against the uniqueness of another, in twos. Then double the numbers and end up with a mass of touching fingertips.

Invention

OBJECTIVE

Co-operative fun game

NUMBERS

All

EQUIPMENT

None

DETAILS

Everyone in groups of 10 or so.
Each group decides on a machine or vehicle which they are to become, e.g. tractor, juke box, pinball machine, washing machine, or anything dug from the imagination. Give time for discussion. They construct it themselves.

NOTES

It's good to video each one then show them all to applause and laughter.

?	?	√

Body Swop

OBJECTIVE

Good spectator stunt for fun

NUMBERS

3 couples

EQUIPMENT

3 large jackets/shirts or vests – as big as possible

DETAILS

The male dresses in clothes which are inside out and in incorrect order:

    Jacket 1st
    Shirt 2nd
.   Vest 3rd

The couple holds hands. Then, while still holding hands, they exchange the clothing from each other.

The girls should end up with the clothes on in the correct order.

NOTES

Good party fun game.

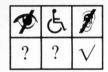

Banana Relay

OBJECTIVE

Participative fun

NUMBERS

Any number of couples

EQUIPMENT

1 banana for every 2 people.

DETAILS

This game is as much fun to watch as it is to play.
Prepare a course to run (e.g. between chairs), and on "Go" each couple peels a banana, holds it between them in their mouths, and runs together around the course. On their return the next 2 people peel their banana and so on. The objective is to race without breaking the banana.

SPECIAL NOTES

It can be played in teams and scored to create a competition – but fun should be the main motivator.
Alternative: try the same with a tomato between foreheads!

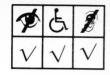

Gloved Gum Game

OBJECTIVE

Team fun, fiddly game

NUMBERS

2 or more teams

EQUIPMENT

A carrier bag and a pair of gardening gloves for each team. Bubble gum for each person.

DETAILS

Divide your group into 2 or more teams. Give each team a pair of gloves and a carrier bag containing sticks of gum. On "Go" the first person in each team puts on the gloves, grabs a piece of gum from the bag and unwraps it using only his or her teeth and hands. Then he or she begins chewing the gum and passes the bag to the next person. The winner is the first team to have everyone blowing bubbles.

String Dance

OBJECTIVE

Fun – group cohesiveness game

NUMBERS

All – as equipment permits

EQUIPMENT

1 big ball of string (allow 4 to 5 feet per player)
1 large metal spoon

DETAILS

Tie the spoon to one end of the piece of string and get all the players to form a line or a circle (better). Hand the spoon to the first person in the line, who must then thread it through their clothing, e.g. up the trouser leg and out through the shirt. The spoon and string are then passed to the next in line and goes down the blouse, down the waist of the skirt, and then up the trouser leg of the next person. Each player does the same until each person is 'sewn' to the next. Then the string is unthreaded, but this time by the person next to each player.

SPECIAL NOTES

Great party game. You can't imagine the spontaneous behaviour! It's great with a really big group – and a very cold metal spoon! (Try the fridge!!)

No Teeth

OBJECTIVE

Fun

NUMBERS

The whole group

EQUIPMENT

None

DETAILS

Here's one of those "you only lose when you laugh" games.
Have your group sit in a circle. From this point forward, you may not show your teeth. To speak, you pull your lips inward around your teeth to hide them.
One member starts by asking the person next to him, "Is Mrs Mangle home?"
The person responds, "I don't know – I'll have to ask my neighbour."
This keeps going around the circle. When someone's teeth show due to laughter, he's out. Smiling is permitted provided the teeth don't show. When asking or answering, contorting the facial muscles may be used to try to "crack up" the person next to you.
When the group narrows to the strong ones, it's good to re-arrange the sitting order to weed out any "closet laughter".

👁	♿	🏃
?	?	√

Tombstone

OBJECTIVE

Fun self-description game or exercise

NUMBERS

3 couples

EQUIPMENT

3 big drawings of tombstones
Large black felt-tip pens or paint and brushes

DETAILS

One from each couple holds the big tombstone drawing. The others write down what they would like to appear on their tombstone, e.g., "Here lies . . . he had good looks, big nose, lived for . . . achieved . . ." and so on, touching on character, personality, work etc.
The imagination will flow!

SPECIAL NOTES

This can also be done using small pieces of paper in a group context.
As an alternative, write a "For Sale" advert for yourself or your partner.

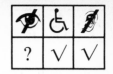

Laugh Machine

OBJECTIVE

A good fun laughing time

NUMBERS

All in groups of 5 or 6

EQUIPMENT

Design and build a Laugh Machine – basically something big and colourful with a large handle and light or buzzer – let the imagination be savage with a tea-chest and a battery and door-bell concoction.

DETAILS

Try it in teams first, one at a time, then with the whole group together.
When the handle goes down and the light is on, everyone laughs.
When the handle is up and the light off, everyone stops laughing.
Individuals drop out if they laugh at the wrong time.

NOTES

It's boring but you can use a raised hand instead of the Laugh Machine.
You will find people laughing at laughing – it's infectious.
Expect a chaotic ending!

Snake Tails

OBJECTIVE

Energetic fun team game

NUMBERS

All in groups 6–10 players

EQUIPMENT

Handkerchief per team

DETAILS

Each group forms a "snake" by players holding the waist of the person in front (except for the first person, of course). The last person in the "snake" tucks a handkerchief under his belt at the back to form a tail.

On the signal to start, each snake attempts to grab the tails from the other snakes without losing their own. Only the head of each snake can make the grabs. The more snakes, the more hilarious the "pile-up" result.

End with one big group doing a Group Hug (see page 200).

SPECIAL NOTES

Try bigger and bigger lines/teams until it becomes chaotic fun.

Lifting the Pyramid

OBJECTIVE

Fun

NUMBERS

Individuals or teams

EQUIPMENT

Clean paper serviettes or paper handkerchiefs

DETAILS

The handkerchief is unfolded and arranged in a pyramid shape and placed on the floor about 12 to 18 inches away from the feet of the competitor, who is then told to stand on one leg, bend down, pick up the handkerchief with the teeth and recover to standing position without losing balance.

The foot on which they are balancing must not move, nor must their hands touch the ground.

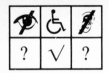

No laugh

OBJECTIVE

Good fun

NUMBERS

All present in groups – minimum 8 to 10 per group

EQUIPMENT

None

DETAILS

Get everyone into circular groups of about 8–10, standing or sitting.
Teach everyone this saying as if they were 5-year-old kids: "I think you are very attractive and very funny but I'm not going to laugh."
Then get one member to start and pass on the saying around the group, with top and bottom lips pulled tighter over the top of the teeth.
The aim is to go around the circle without anyone laughing.

NOTES

Expect much laughter and don't bother with "success" as long as everyone has a go.
If appropriate get the best (i.e. funniest) from each group to come on stage and say the saying over the microphone.
You could make up your own appropriate "topical" or "in" phrase.

Crazy Chase

NUMBERS

All present, as many as possible

EQUIPMENT

Pens
Leaflets as below
Piece of paper

DETAILS

Give each person a 'Crazy Chase' list, plus a pen or pencil. On "Go" they follow the instructions on the list – and the first back is the winner.

CRAZY CHASE LIST

Each stunt to be signed by another participant – NOT YOU. You must assist others if asked.

1. Get ten different autographs. First and last names in full.
2. Unlace someone's shoe, lace it, and tie it again. (Not your own) ....
3. Get a hair over six inches long from someone's head. (Let *them* remove it.) ....
4. Get a girl to do a somersault and sign her name here ......
5. Have a boy do five push-ups for you and sign his name here ....
6. Play "Ring a Ring of Roses" with someone and sing out loud. ....
7. Do twenty five jumps from "at ease" to "attention", and back again, saluting each time. Have someone count them for you ....

8. Sing the National Anthem (first verse only) to someone ...
9. Leapfrog over someone five times ....
10. Buy an icecream cornet and ask someone to push it in your face ....

SPECIAL NOTES

Add to your own crazy list but don't make it too long – just crazy!

Knee Knee

OBJECTIVE

Good fun, good party game

NUMBERS

Groups of 5 to 10 people

EQUIPMENT

None

DETAILS

Everyone sits around in a circle on the floor, crosslegged or seated on chairs. Each person places his or her hands on the knees of the people on either side. This makes a network of crossed hands – every knee has someone else's hand on it.

A pat on the knee is passed around the circle. This is difficult at first, becomes easier, but is always good fun.

Anyone who does two pats on someone's knee reverses the direction around the circle. This can franticise the game once people get used to it.

Give the game a good run this way. Then do a knockout. When anyone goes wrong, that hand drops out. Everyone stays in the circle until the last two hands remain. Winning is less important than the fun.

You can do it with feet instead!

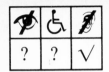

Body Balloons

OBJECTIVE

Loads of fun

NUMBERS

Any number in twos

EQUIPMENT

One balloon for each couple

DETAILS

Boy and girl stand facing each other with an inflated balloon between their chests. On "Go" the aim is for the girl to go down and clamber between the legs of the boy whilst keeping the balloon in bodily contact. The balloon will roll with the bodies, the eventual outcome finding the couple standing back to back with the baloon between their backs – or thereabouts.

NOTES

Good game for upfront demo impact for a large event. Good party game, too.
Water balloons add spice!

Visual Games

Introduction to Visuals

THE BLOB TREE in this section has been one of the most used and requested "tools" I've ever developed. It first appeared in my last book *Games Without Frontiers*, and since then I have received numerous requests to use it in other publications and contexts. The original is enclosed plus a new Blob Tree, followed by several other similar "Blob" tools.

As well as being suitable for people who are not literate, they are useful in varied situations. I have found them to be a great opener – opening people up in a non-threatening way, including self-revelation, group awareness, raising awareness of others or our own feelings.

All these are good for use with small groups but they can also be used with large groups, with an overhead projector (O.H.P.) to project the visuals for all to see. The other visuals in this section can be used in similar ways to the Blob Tree. There are advantages in an individual handout, a piece of paper for everyone, a visual to focus upon. They can defuse the eyeball-to-eyeball interactions which can be threatening to some.

SPECIAL NOTE

It is important at the end of any emotionally charged game to allow all participants a period of time to *de-role*. This can be best done by giving each group of three, time to chat these individual feelings through.
De-roling is different to de-briefing.
De-briefing is part of the package of learning from the role play.
De-roling is actually leaving the role behind and affirming 'self' – affirming reality.
For example '*I am* Pip Wilson, I have a wife Joan, daughters Ann and Joy – I have been through the learning experience. I am *not* . . . (whatever role has been played) I am . . . etc.'
If you plan tea or coffee during the evening the best time is now.

98

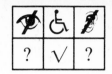

Blob Tree

The many many ways of using it

OBJECTIVE

To facilitate sharing which aids self-understanding, understanding of others and a general awareness. Also a good ice breaker.

NUMBERS

Can be used by two people, small groups or large groups split into smaller groups for sharing.

DETAILS

1. Give out a copy of the Blob Tree or project a copy for all to see, using an overhead projector.
2. Ask them to view and chose which Blob on the tree they FEEL like in a certain group.
3. This could be the group now present, or another group they belong to, e.g. teams of workers, a Church or Youth Club, YMCA, social club, community association – any group.
4. Have them share in threes or fours (larger group sharing is good, but it takes much longer).
5. It can end here – but following are some other methods to enhance the use of this tool.
6. Feedback to whole group. Instead of repeating the information already shared in threes and fours (as above, 4) a fellow member speaks on another's behalf.
7. A development of this, and an alternative, is to have feedback to the whole group in the form of an 'empathy exercise', e.g. Errol and Claudette. Errol speaks, "I am Claudette and my blob was . . ." Done with feeling and an absence of giggles and quips, this can help create a positive, creative climate which could be used developmentally by the group worker.

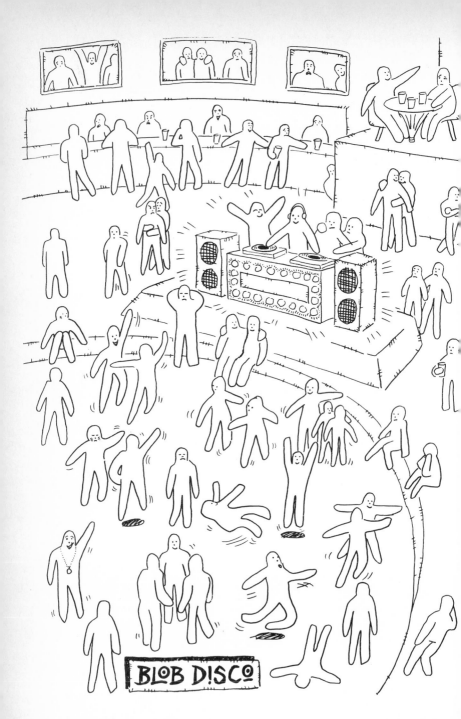

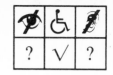

Blob Disco

(See Blob Tree for further detail on general usage)

OBJECTIVE

A communication tool to assist groups of (young?) people to share their feelings

NUMBERS

In twos, small groups or large group using OHP

DETAILS

Distribute a copy of this to everyone present. Pre-select series of questions. Decide to use open discussion in groups or break up into groups of three or four people. (Note: open group discussion with groups of more than five persons can be less valuable than Buzz groups followed by open group sharing.)

SOME QUESTIONS TO STIMULATE DISCUSSION

Q1   What I like to do
Q2   What I like to be
Q3   What I feel like
Q4   What I feel like when I have been drinking
Q5   Which of these Blob persons is feeling "not OK"?
Q6   Which of these Blob persons is most likely to be drug dependent?
Q7   Which of these Blob persons is most likely to be a Christian?
Q8   Which of these Blob persons is most likely to be a Youth Worker?
Q9   If you were part of the group (near bottom to left) how difficult would it be for you to speak to the Blob with arms folded?

Q10 Is it more important to be part of a group all the time or are you able to step away to make relationship contact with some less integrated person?

Q11 Where is God in this Disco?

Q12 What does God want of you, want you to do, in this sort of context?

BLOB WORLD

•BLOB CHURCH~→

•BLOB CONCERT•

AFTER-8-BLOBS

Use as Blob Tree, Blob Disco, Blob Concert
Remember: Posing the Question stimulates the outcome!

SAMPLE QUESTIONS

Which blob do you feel like?
Which blob would you like to be?
Which blob is most like your contribution?
Which blob is most positive in the group/community?
Which blob is most negative in the group/community?

Using Blobs
Get your local artist to draw one which is localised –
most relevant to your own community, activity
group, etc. Draw on A4 (send me a copy for my
nextbook!), paint on a wall, photocopy onto an OHP
acetate and use time and time again. Response is
different every day!

MAKE YOUR OWN

THINK "OUTCOME – NOT ACTIVITY"

Dangerous Thoughts

Dangerous Thoughts

a Standardise
b Freedom
c Beauty

OBJECTIVE

To self-discover in groups using visual aids. To understand that we are bombarded with images, influences and attitudes which are not all good.

NUMBERS

One or more small groups of 5 to 8

EQUIPMENT

Hand out one copy each of the visual aids or display them by overhead projector.

DETAILS

Ask each member to choose one item from the handout and speak to the whole group about it. **a** Is it my attitude? **b** Is it a good/bad attitude? **c** Is it what God desires?

NOTE

These are not easily understood visual aids – that is the challenge. They are not "all on a plate" answers, simplistic. They are designed to be triggers for the mind.

DANGEROUS THOUGHTS

Lessen One: STANDARDISE. IN an Effort

To keep our COLD COMMODITY CULTURE MOVING, CREATIVE THOUGHTS AND PEOPLE R ANARCHISTS!!! RHYMES WITH C....C.

ALL Fashion, Art, Food, TV, Faith, Books, Ideas, Sexuality, Shape, must, let ME repeat repeat MUST CONFIRM

B COOL Ne HOT

WISDOM COMES FROM ABOVE → The manager One K°

stocks + keeps....

NOTE HOW HARD LINES R 4 MEN

"neighbours. everybody needs television"

BUY THESE ideas now → BE AT the CRASSMAS RUSH OVER WORK is good for the SOLE

KEEP YOUR DISTANCE

KEEP YOUR STANCE

NOTHING don't follow THE WORLD follow LIFE.
1
2
3
FULL

Fill every space

WOMEN MUST BE ROUND + SOFT, BRAINLESS + PREGNANT. THE ALTERNATIVE IS LESBIANISM OR 2 BECOME MALE + AGGRESSIVE?

POSE in CLOTHES

1960's LIBERATED LEVEL

1990's SEXY LEVEL

don't think just no

This year UR THIN Next year UR An Arec-sick

Confused? BUY THE FACELESS Loos YOUR SELF (see freud)

Remember 2 FORGET

DANGER-I-US
TH@UGHTS

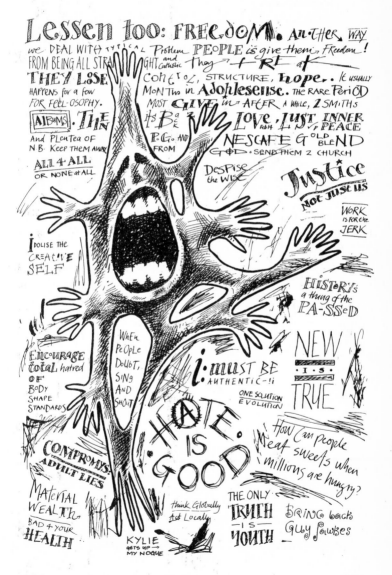

Lessen 100: FREEDOM. An-ther WAY we DEAL WITH TYPICAL Problem PEOPLE is give them Freedom! FROM BEING ALL STRAIGHT and catholic They + RE at THEY LOSE cohЕrOL, STRUCTURE, hope. It usually HAPPENS for a few MoNThs in Adohlesensc. The RARE PeriOD FOR Feel-OSOPHY. MOST GIVE in AFTER A while, 2 SMiTHs

ALBUMS. The IN Is Back

LOVE FroM JUST INNER PEACE

And PLENTEA OF N.B. Keep them AWAY FROM P G AND

NESCAFE GOLD BLEND GOD. SEND them 2 CHURCH

ALL 4 ALL OR NONE at ALL

DESPISE the WISE

JUSTICE NOT JUST US

WORK IS FOR the JERK

iDOLISE THE CREATIVE SELF

HISTORY's a thing of the PA-SSED

ENCOURAGE total hatred OF BODY SHAPE STANDARDS

WHEN PeOPLE DOUBT, SING AND SHOUT

i MUST BE AUTHENTIC-!i

ONE SOLUTION EVOLUTION

NEW ·IS· TRUE

HATE IS GOOD

How Can People eat sweets when millions are hungry?

COMPROMYS ADULT LIES

MATERIAL WEALTH BAD 4 YOUR HEALTH

think Globally Act Locally

THE ONLY TRUTH IS YOUTH

BRING back GUY FAWKES

KYLIE GETS UP MY NOGUE

DANGEROUS Thoughts

Re-BoRN Free: BEAUTY. WhAt is PeRHAPS SURPRISING—We don't K-NO-W WHAT beauty iS. SOCieTY TeLLS us it is YOUTHFUL LOOKS—YET GOD has made us ALL, examples of HIS precious HANDY WORK. We R ALL Reflections of ASPeCTS of God—IN HIS BEAUTI-FULL IMAGE.

SHALLOW MINDS think that BeaUTY IS ONLY SKIN DEEP

U may not B MUNROE 2 the media but U R SPECIAL TO GOD

LOOK BEYOND LOOKS

BEAUTY is in the eye of the CREATOR →

THE HEART IS WHERE WE SHOULD START →

WORDS CREATE INNER BeauTeA

GOD ONLY CREATES BEAUTY FOLLOW HIM

Quarter Pages

Each of the ideas on the following pages can be photocopied and folded into a folder/leaflet/handout. Several options for use are suggested here.

Please feel free to photocopy and use as you wish.* Think sensitively of your group and the context. You know your group best – be adventurous. Deliver them in a size, form and quantity appropriate to your group.

*Although all rights are reserved by the author and artist, we are willing to authorise photocopying in limited numbers, and use on overhead projectors, for activity groups only, on the understanding that full credit to the source is always given.

Using the Invite Folder

OPTION A   INVITE FOLDER METHOD

1. Photocopy any single quarter page onto A4 paper. Fold into booklet form.
2. Hand-write or type on inside pages your own personal Invite to the session (meeting, evening, after-eight group meeting, camp discussion).
3. Hand out to members or prospective members.

OPTION B   GROUP HANDOUT FOLDER METHOD

1. Photocopy any page onto A4 and fold to make a 4-page photocopy folder.
2. Hand out to group members. Here are some options:

   a Ask for quietness and have members write two comments on each leaf as they read: first, an instant feeling towards the page; second, an instant thought towards the page. Then get each person to share their thoughts and feelings.

   b Get everyone into threes before giving out the folders. Ask for two minutes discussion on page one (only). Then get feedback from whole group. Then do other pages.

NOTE

Working in threes is good. It allows for silent/quiet members, it defuses the overpowering individual a little, it helps sex mix dynamics, it is less threatening than twos.

Go through each page like this, i.e. small groups of three first, followed by large group.

OPTION C POSTER METHOD

1. Photocopy each picture to large size (A3).
2. Display each one in turn, asking for comment/discussion.

OPTION D (BLESSED ARE THE RICH Etc. IDEA)

Spot the difference.

NOTES

Group learning versus an individual teaching. Humans in groups can learn so much. There is so much experience and knowledge in a group, far more than in any one individual – even you. The group leader needs to pull out the feelings, thoughts, values and beliefs of the group members. The Group Leader can share, too. No put-downs, please. Don't build up your own views by opposing other views.

Tips on leading discussion on sensitive issues (in fact any issues). Ask everyone to comment. Never press anyone to comment. Always thank individuals following their comment – on every occasion. Never follow their comments with a negative comment of your own. No put-downs.

Banner Making

Use any of the visuals to make banners to suit your particular context(s). Some ideas:

BEDSHEETS

Re-draw the visual on to bedsheets. A simple coat of white emulsion paint will provide a good surface for pencil outlines, followed by felt-tip pen outlines or, better still, vivid emulsion paints.

ENLARGING PICTURES

Draw half-inch squares all over your master copy.
Draw the same number of squares all over your bedsheet using equal numbers and squareness.
Transfer the detail from each small square to each large square – bingo, you have a banner.

Being positive – creating a climate

Having powerful quotations, provocative quotations and holistic statements are positive ICONS in a world producing many negative icons.

Pic, Mix and Discuss

Photocopy each of the visuals on pages 118 to 138. Place them all in a hat (or converted litter bin) in the centre of your group. Each member picks one.

Quietly and confidentially each person writes on it a personal experience in his or her life which is triggered into mind by the visual. All return their visuals to the hat.

Pick and mix continues by each group member picking one from the hat and in turn reading aloud the quote on the visual, followed by the hand-written personal comment.

Adapt this to suit your own group needs. The objective suggested is to create open reaction with a view to stimulating feelings and developing thoughts.

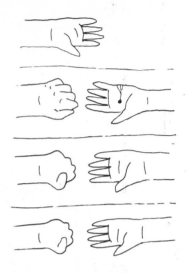

Take up your cross and follow me...

← Jesus?

...hey, I was only joking man.

← ?

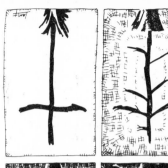

Celebrate ★ Christing

Cash-mas...
Crush-mas...
Cost-mas...
Crass-mas...

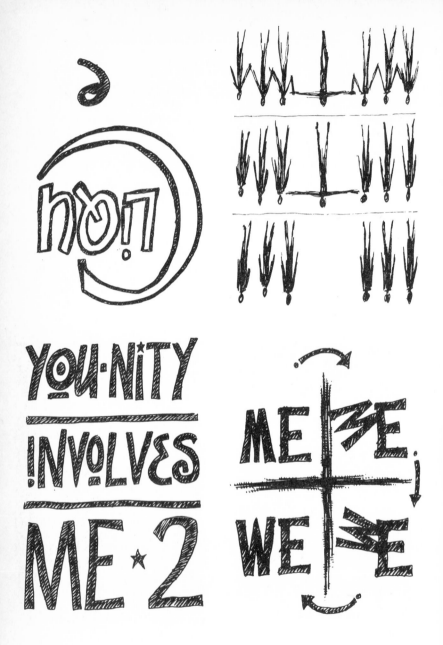

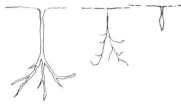

2 eyes R BETTER THAN ONE

SHALLOW MINDS ONLY LOOK SKIN DEEP

APART -HEID

The wise still SEEK HIM...

122

WHO CONTROLS the→ PAST CONTROLS the→ FUTURE

‹VIEWS·PAPERS

DAILY TORYGRAPH§ *The Independent of Maxwell + Murdoch*

Nudes of the World THE SIN‹ Daily MALE›

THE ST★R *wise people don't follow it* SUNDAY PORN

TORY

JESUS
MAN OF SORROWS, CRUCIFIED, HATED + FEARED

20TH © CHRISTIAN
HAPPY, RICH, SUCCESSFUL, LOVED AND RESPECTED

HISTORY
HERSTORY
WHO'S STORY?

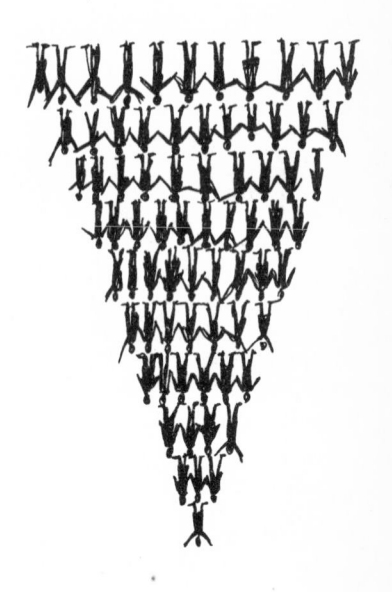

¿GOD?
CLEAR
WHAT

WE THINK WE
KNOW GOD...

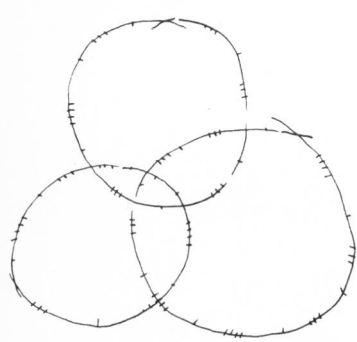

YET HAVEN'T A CLUE
ABOUT OURSELVES!

...WHERE U
FIND TREASURE

X
MARKS the
SPOT...

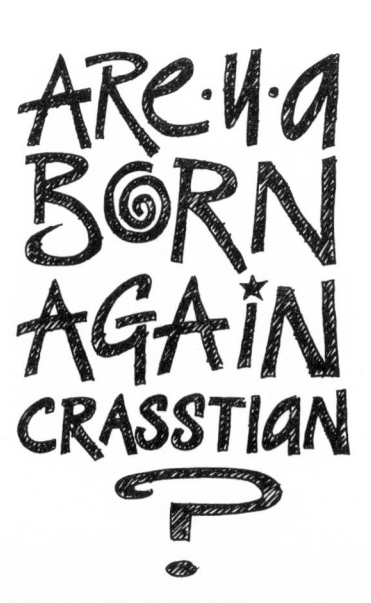

ARE·U·a
BORN
AGAIN
CRASSTIAN
?

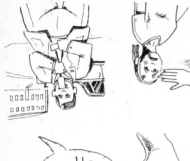

THE WORLD GO ROUND THE BEND — MONEY MAKES

BLESSED R THE RICH
WOE·2·THE POOR

STOP THE THIRD WORLD WAR

126

THE MORE I LISTEN I NEED TO UNDERSTAND THE MORE I LISTEN LISTEN

We're afraid of SILENCE
We'd have too much time to THINK

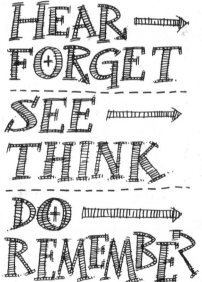

HEAR ⟶
FORGET
SEE ⟶
THINK
DO ⟶
REMEMBER

NOISE ANNOYS

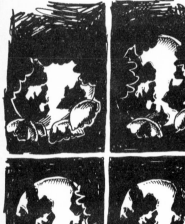

HOW DO U .
COPE WITH
THE FACT
THAT ½ THE
STARVE

SHALOM

Justice
→ not ←
Just Us

WHERE WE
LIVE
AFFECTS
WHAT WE
BELIEVE

WHAT MARK DO YOU?
LEAVE WITH PEOPLE!

THOSE
WHO CAN'T
DANCE
SAY THE
BEAT IS
EVIL

HEROES FRIENDS
PARENTS
ADVERTS T.V.
ME

SELF-PORTRAIT?

SHARING WEALTH is GOOD 4 YOUR HEALTH

Smile - Jesus loves you.

It takes more than rain + sun to make a harvest...

...it takes more than rain + sun to make a drought.

1st

3RD

u-R
You-nique

BITTON
I-AM

V·I·P's

BE-
YOU
-TY

MOTHER THERESA | MARTIN L-KING | YOU!

132

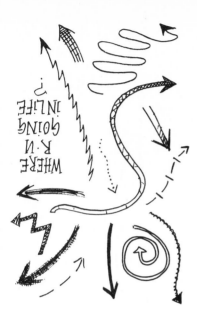

FASHION
BACK IN
PASSION
LETS RIT

DONT B
COOL
B
HOT

PEOPLE DON'T
LIVE OR DIE
PEOPLE JUST
FLOAT

WHAT·ARE·U·DOING WiTH·IT?

TiME...

Televisi·OFF

BACK2LiFE BACK2REALiTY

THERE'S MORE 2 LIFE THAN DYING

ONLY ONE PERSON IN THE HOUSE CAN INTEREST EVERYONE 4 OVER AN HOUR

HOLLOW

THE

SWALLOW

DON'T

AS DIFFERENT AS EAST+WEST

BEWARE

AWARE

B

ADVERTISING
STINKS

MOST OF US
Like THE
SMELL

'NOISE'

135

FAITH
FULL
NESS.

PAWN
OGRAPHY

MAKING
LOVE
STARTS WITH
THE GOOD
MORNING
KISS

GIVE US
THIS DAY
OUR DAILY
KISS

THE GOD WHOSE HANDS

MADE EVERY TREE

WAS BORN AS MAN

TO SET US FREE

NIGHT IS WHEN YOUR LITTLE LIGHT IS SEEN

TO TRY + TO FAIL IS NOT LAZINESS

— SIERRA LEONE PROVERB

SOMETIMES THE ONLY WAY FORWARD IS TO TAKE ONE STEP BACK

Bits and Pieces

Official R.M. Paper

Give out copies of the Official Rolling Magazine Paper (page 140) to each person at the start of the weekend, session or day (whatever). Give two minutes for them to decide what to do with their individual sheet.

You may need to suggest a broad range of uses – the full spectrum, from ripping it up to creating delicate, beautiful things.

After two minutes each human is asked to mill around with other humans sharing why they did what they did to the paper. The group leader then explains: "This weekend (or event) is just like the Official Rolling Magazine Paper. You can freely choose what you do with it – destroy, mutilate, or be creative." End of illustration. This point needs to be expanded, obviously, in a way that *your* group members can understand. Think before the start how best to make things clear.

Parts of the Body

This is a discussion starter needing much sensitivity.
Teenagers are often more sensitive about their bodies than older
or younger people.

PHASE 1

Everyone in your group receives a photocopy of the Bits and
Pieces page (page 146). A Poem can be read to stimulate thinking and set the climate.
Get everyone to talk in groups of threes around the room.
(Groups of threes are often better than twos. A different
dynamic is set. A larger group often takes much longer to reach
real sharing.)
Each person chooses a body part he or she feels good about
and says why. Then the large group hears the answers. Be
sensitive and allow laughter and embarrassed fun, but recognise
avoidance and bring the group back to the task. Never force
sharing. Always offer an easy way out. Encourage, however,
earnestly encourage people to take risks in sharing.

PHASE 2

Threes again. Each person chooses the body part he or she
would like to swop for another. Then back in the large group
again to hear the answers. Some wonderfully sensitive sharing
can go on here.
(Usually, everyone has a least preferred body part – legs, teeth,
nose, etc. Often it has not been shared with anyone. It can be
a liberating experience to do this.)
Conclude by reading the poem again or share thoughts on how
God loves us as we are. Emphasise how it is important to
"own" our own body – not to go through life saying or thinking
"If Only!"

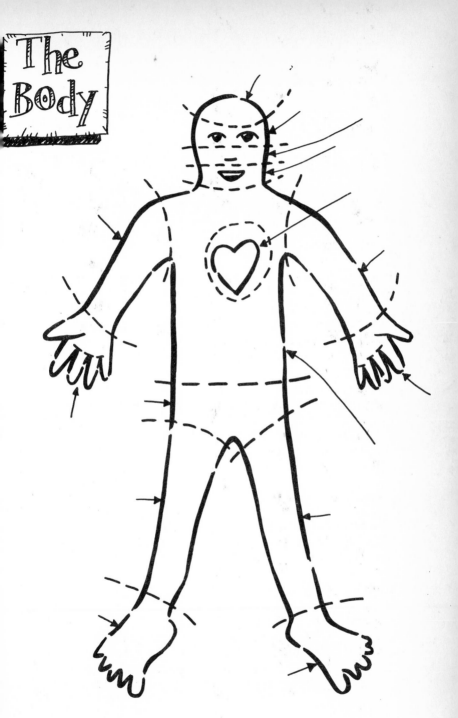

The Body

143

Limbs of the Body

OBJECTIVE

To raise self-awareness relating to role in community group or church.

OPTION ONE

This can be an ice-breaker before a meeting or group activity. Each group member receives a photocopy of the Limbs Page (page 143).

Read from the Bible and/or a poem to stimulate thought and raise awareness.

1. BIBLE
1 Corinthians Chapter 12 verses 12 to 26
2. POEM
Find your own. Suggest Games Without Frontiers, Poems chapter (i) Each person shares in groups of 3, which limb would describe the role they play in the group, their community or society in general, i.e. hand = reaches out; eye = watching, aware; heart = generous, warm (ii) Each person describes the limb which they *feel* (it can be different from the one they see as their role).

OPTION TWO

Each person has a photocopy of the Limbs Page, and is asked to share the following in groups of three:

Which do they feel, depending on their highs and lows?
When do they feel vulnerable?
Which limb they would like to be?
Which would they hate to be?

OPTION THREE (Using large copy of "The Body")

Conclude in the large group. Each individual is given a bright stick-on label of some sort. They walk up to an enlarged copy of The Body (p. 143) stick the label onto the limb they feel they are, as part of this group (i.e. youth group, church, worker team).

End with recognition/discussion: and a suitable reflective reading?

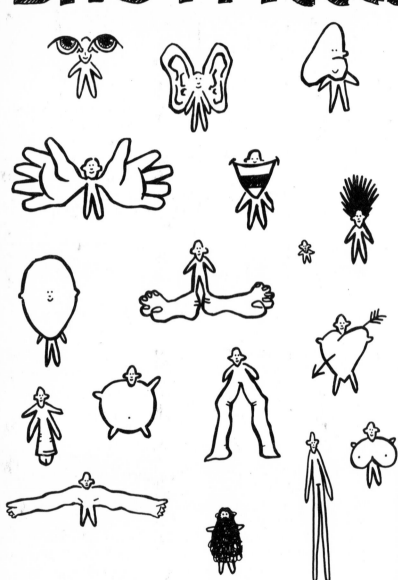

Affirmation Sheet

OBJECTIVE

To end a weekend, conference or session of some sort in a positive way. To be affirmative – a blessing for all concerned.

NOTE

This is serious. Needs to be handled in a climate where people will respond and follow tasks. It can be ruined by frivolity.

NUMBERS

All

EQUIPMENT

For each participant:
A photocopy of the BHP (Beautiful Human Person) Affirmation Sheet (page 149)
A straight pin – sewing type (ouch!)
A small felt-tip pen (ball point pens/pencils not as good)

DETAILS

The hard work and activity of a weekend/training day/evening has almost ended. Introduce this game by saying it is the "close down" session. A time to build each other up in a world full of knocks and bruises.
Ask the group to collect a BHP sheet, a pin and a felt-tip pen each. Get them to pin the sheets on each other's backs. Each

person needs to go to every other group member and write one word or one sentence on each person's back, such as:

Something which you value about that person
Something which you feel about that person
Something which you appreciate about that person
Some characteristic which contributes to life

It can refer to body, mind, spirit, personality, dress, attitudes, anything – but it must be *affirmative*.

Allow the group to mill until, hopefully, everyone has written on everyone else's back. During the last few minutes ask participants *not* to remove their paper until you indicate.

Finally, ask them all to remove their BHP sheets and read them in silence.

Use of silence in a group:
Often silence can be used to heighten feelings and touch deeper issues inside a person. When people's feelings are stirred, often they will laugh, joke, talk, shout, etc. with embarrassment. The use of silence can raise awareness and stimulate development if handled well by the group facilitator.

Allow prolonged stillness in the room. Then quietly ask the group to identify the following:

1. A feeling. One word which describes their feeling at the moment.
2. The statement on the paper which stands out most for any reason.
3. The one which puzzles them the most.
4. The one which creates uneasiness or negativeness.
5. The one which makes them feel good.

Then, and only then, ask individuals to share one of the above publicly.

Use the above words as a guide. You know your group best. Adjust the words appropriately for *them*.

Good, eh! If you doubt its usefulness, try it. It is one of the best group experiences – it's Kingdomful.

YOU·R·A·
BEAUTY
→ FULL ←
HUMAN ↑
PERSON ↘

Butterfly

OBJECTIVES

Building up one another. Affirmation. Speaking the truth in love even if it's embarrassing.

NUMBERS

Any number in small groups of 5 to 8. It can be played in larger groups with careful facilitation.

EQUIPMENT

For each person:
A pen or pencil
A photocopy of the BHP (Beautiful Human Person) Butterfly (page 152)

DETAILS
OPTION ONE

They all get a copy of the Butterfly sheet and write their name on it. Then the papers are passed around the circle and each person adds a comment: "what makes that named person beautiful", one thing that you appreciate about this person – it could be something they have done, a physical attribute, personality, character, etc.
When the paper has passed around the full circle you ask the group to read in quietness and then share their thoughts in turn (similar to the last game).

OPTION TWO

Instead of passing around the circle, all the group put their Butterfly sheets into a centrally placed litter bin and then pick them out randomly in a mix and pic technique (see Note). Each person writes a comment on a sheet, then they are returned to the bin before being passed to their owners.

NOTE

Mix and Pic: This is a good method to distribute papers if you want to encourage individuals to comment anonymously about one another. All the papers go into a bin in the centre of the group and are picked out at random.

Group Games

Pip's Intro

FEELINGS GAMES

When games involve role play or any form of experiencing feelings there must always be time given to what the training professionals call de-roling.

At one training weekend that I was involved with a young woman played a role for less than one minute, which included violence and aggression. She carried those intense feelings for the rest of the weekend because she wasn't de-roled. That is bad news in a context which is intending to be a 'good news' learning experience.

DE-ROLING

Get all involved in the feelings experience to
1. Spend time talking about those feelings in a small group of people who they are familiar with and trust.
2. Have them talk freely about their feelings in the role play. Then look at the role from outside and analyse what had happened when 'in role'.

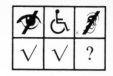

Hand Dance

OBJECTIVE

Non-threatening, non-verbal communication to build awareness.

NUMBERS

Everyone present in twos.

EQUIPMENT

None

DETAILS

Explain this is a non-verbal game using the hands only.
Everyone sits on the floor in twos facing each other with eyes closed. They touch both hands together, then, following the leader's instructions, they express with their hands. The following are some suggestions.
End by discussing feelings and anything learned from the game.

Greet each other	Make up
Do rock 'n' roll dance	Give a kiss
Play together	Give support
Fight	Counsel one another
Accept each other	Repeat any of the above or add new
Reject each other	ones
	End – say goodbye

Circle of Massage

OBJECTIVE

Group relaxation, affirmation towards building a climate of trust and openness.

NUMBERS

In groups of 6 to 15 (aim for about 10)

EQUIPMENT

None

DETAILS

Everyone stands in a circle. Ask everyone to turn, and put their left shoulder pointing into the centre. Everyone put their left hand up high. Everyone put their right hand up high
Gently bring down the left hand onto the left shoulder of the person in front, and then the right.
On the word "Go" everyone gently massages the shoulder of the person in front – the emphasis is on gentleness and it being a positive not negative experience.

NOTES

People can accept this in the middle of a session of other games, when they are relaxed and not apprehensive of each other.
It can also be played sitting down – with eyes open or closed – with music—gently patting – and praying too!
This activity, when done without eye contact, can be a real acceptance activity and one which builds group cohesiveness.

Palm Person

OBJECTIVE

Self-observation aided by group analysis of communication styles.

NUMBERS

Groups of 6 to 10

EQUIPMENT

A pen or pencil and a Palm Person ranking sheet for each person (page 160)

DETAILS

1. Distribute a copy of the ranking sheet to everyone.
2. All study and mark themselves avoiding the middle ground (please!).
3. Then each person chooses one number as their number one priority to work on for their own development.
4. Then, in the whole group, look at the number each individual chose, and the group suggests the ranking they would give – and they say why. This facilitates the process of self-analysis followed by group analysis.

NOTES

Affirmation builds up.
Criticism, even the constructive, and gently-handled kind, can destroy or undermine an individual. The group analysis needs careful, sensitive handling.
For more on the Palm Person, see page 29.

Palm Person Ranking Sheet

Describe yourself by marking each one

Closed Palms

1. Withholding, revealing little, silent or making trivial communication

2. Carefully considered, cautious, safe, filtered responses

3. Superficial, false communications, avoidance of controversy

4. Ignoring others, avoiding relationships

5. Prejudging others, stereotyping

6. Giving advice, offering quick or easy solutions

7. Being too much controlled by "shoulds" and "oughts"

8. "If only this . . . if only that"

9. Generalising
"Everyone . . ."
"They . . ."
"We all . . ."

Open Palms

1. Responding to others with openess, initiating meeting relating

2. Spontaneous giving, offering reactions not interpretations

3. Authentic communication expressing real feelings and real thoughts, exploring differences

4. Ready to offer both support and confrontation

5. Listening carefully, sensitive to spoken and unspoken messages, showing empathy

6. Showing interest, clarifying, trusting the other to decide

7. Accepting self and accepting responsibility for decisions

8. Accepting the situation, working on it

9. Keeping comments specific. Use of "I" rather than "we"

10. "There and then" –
talking about outside
issues

10. "Here and now" –
talking about *our*
relationships

11. Theorising as an escape
from relationships

11. Staying close to
relationships even when
uncomfortable

12. Disowning parts of self
which embarrass, avoiding
how *I* feel

12. Being in touch with,
aware of and ready to talk
about feelings as well as
ideas

13. Defensive, rejecting
what others offer

13. Open to learn about
myself

14. Too many observations
to the whole group

14. Directing specific
comments to particular
persons

15. Vague, tentative
comments and
suggestions, backing off
too easily if opposed

15. Clear messages and
requests. Letting others
know what *I* want or where
I stand

Robin Hood

A really good game I've used for years.

OBJECTIVE

To create an interesting and gripping debate in small groups
with a view to raising awareness in the following areas:
Group dynamics – how a group functions.
Roles – how individuals relate in groups
Sex roles – individual attitudes to males and females.
Feelings – awareness raising, understanding own and other peo-
ple's feelings.
There are other benefits too.

NUMBERS

One or more groups of eight. Groups should be not smaller
than 5 or larger than 10.

EQUIPMENT

A piece of paper and pen for each person

DETAILS

1. Get everyone into groups, seated in circles with pen and
   paper.
2. Explain they are about to begin a task which must be
   achieved by the group working together.
3. Ask for quietness – no talking during introductions. Explain
   there will be no questions allowed once the game begins –
   from now on.
4. Read the story below. Twice. Slowly.
5. Each individual must make a list of the characters in the
   story in order of who is worst. Do it confidentially and

quickly. Allow only a minute.

Ensure everyone has done it without slowing the pace of the gathering and losing interest.

6. Then give the task: The group must make one list of the four characters in order – the worst is number one and so on. It must be a group decision by discussion and consensus. The whole group needs to agree the list, with no horse trading ("I'll say this if you say that" sort of idea); no voting to decide the order; no giving points to each and calculating the order.

   Tell them they have 15 minutes and say "Go".

7. Observe the group yourself: list, see, read every movement.

8. In the last 5 minutes, put the pressure on, tell them there are only 5 minutes left and the group *must* achieve the task.

9. 3 minutes to go. Tell them the group must achieve the task, must come up with a list otherwise the whole event will be ruined.

10. On time up, check if any of the groups have not finished. Allow an extra minute or so to enable them to complete.

11. Ask everyone to sit in silence as they finish. Very important.

12. Ask everyone individually to write one word on their paper which describes their feelings right now. Keep the room free of laughter, silly talk, moving around.

13. The game is over. The benefits will now depend on you and how well you can draw out the groups and individuals. One good early step is to get the ones whose "individual list" matched the final "group list" to raise their hands. Be sensitive, but if appropriate, ask others present to note the smug grins on the faces of those with hands raised.

14. Spend much time encouraging people to talk about their *feelings*. Expressing them. Listening to them, too! Other areas to touch on are: the leadership of the group, the roles played, the quietest, noisiest, etc. Input your own observations, too.

15. Only in conclusion do you need to discuss the story issues, i.e. attitudes to Maid Marion because she is a woman, and the men because of the stereotyping and the labels we attach, etc.

16. A suggestion to end the activity is to allow everyone in the room to have one final concluding comment.

THE STORY

The Sheriff of Nottingham captured Little John and Robin Hood and imprisoned them in his maximum security dungeon. Maid Marion begged the Sheriff for their release, pleading her love for Robin.

The Sheriff agreed to release them only if Maid Marion spent the night with him. With some considerable sadness, she at last agreed.

The next morning, the Sheriff released his prisoners. Robin at once demanded that Marion tell him how she persuaded the Sheriff to let them go free.

Marion confessed the truth, and was bewildered when Robin abused her, calling her a slut, and saying he never wanted to see her again.

At this Little John defended her, inviting her to leave Sherwood with him, and promising her his life-long devotion. She accepted and they rode away together.

High/Low

OBJECTIVE

To facilitate group members in assessing and understanding their own stage of development in various areas of life.

NUMBERS

All present

EQUIPMENT

None

DETAILS

Play this game at a point in the life of the group when a climate of trust is established. Take it to a level which is socially acceptable within your group.

Ask participants to sit (ideally on the floor). Explain that this game needs the openness and honesty to be effective. The benefits are personal to individuals. Also that the game entails participants standing or sitting or somewhere in between. Examples: sit, kneel, crouch, half-standing, standing, fully stretched.

First ask everyone present to indicate with their body positions how they feel about the Prime Minister.

(Example: Standing with arms lifted high would indicate fully positive. Lying down flat – totally negative.

Now use other non-threatening topics from the list below. Develop the subjects to a level which is more difficult and exposing. Take the game to a level which you know is acceptable.

TOPICS

Feelings about:

Prime Minister
T.V. Soap (name it)
Their school/college/work
Christmas
This event (weekend, training course, camp, etc.)

Relationship with:

Family (be careful – not everyone has a mother/father)
Friends
Opposite sex
Church
Spiritual life
God
Jesus

Add your own topics – make them relevant and up-to-date.
End. Discuss in small groups or lead into another appropriate activity.

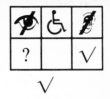

Silhouettes

OBJECTIVE

To encourage a group to affirm one another and build each other up.

EQUIPMENT

Large piece of paper and felt tip pen for each player
A projector (e.g. slide, cine, film projector)

NUMBERS

Ideal 8–15.

DETAILS

1. Pin large pieces of paper around the walls, one for every person.
2. Project the power light on to each person's head in turn while someone draws the silhouette outline on the paper.
3. The group then spend some time writing inside each "head" single words of appreciation of that person. They express what they think about that person.
4. When complete – discussion. The group move around to each picture. At one's own silhouette that person responds to the words written, perhaps picking one really positive one and one which puzzles a little.
5. The activity can be developed: write a positive comment on silhouette arms relating to the practicality of that person (how helpful, skills the person has, etc.)

NOTES

Don't drag it out. Finish when going well.

ALTERNATIVES

If a longer period of time is available, i.e. a weekend, instead of words written on the full-body silhouettes, colour magazines can be cut up and glued all over to form a multi-coloured jumpsuit. The picture will need explaining by the glue person!

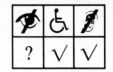

50p

OBJECTIVE

Fun with awareness raising.

NUMBERS

Four people, or any number in fours.

EQUIPMENT

For each group of four: table, chairs, sweets for prizes and 50 pence.

DETAILS

This is a non-verbal game. NO TALKING. It needs to be led well and with the objective in mind.

Place a 50p piece in the table centre and ask participants each to place one index finger on it. On "Go", the participants are to push the coin across the table. When it touches the far edge of the table a sweetie prize is given by the leader.

Watch the game, watch the conflict, give sweets silently/quickly, shushing people quiet. Play for only one minute or so.

Then, with a few words, do a demonstration with one other briefed colleague. Sit either side of the table facing each other, and in a quick smooth operation push the coin quickly from side to side saying, "one sweet – one sweet, two sweets – two sweets," etc.

This non-verbal demo shows clearly how co-operation facilitates a win-win experience. There are benefits for all – sweeties – but the whole principle can be applied to life.

Discuss.

NOTES

Possibly the best way to play this – but you know your group, you decide – is when four people play and the rest of your group sit and observe. Don't drag out either, the game or the application.

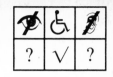

Top Three

OBJECTIVE

Self-awareness exercise.

NUMBERS

Any number, in twos.

EQUIPMENT

Paper and pen for each person.

DETAILS

On the paper supplied (approx. 5 inch square) each person draws a large circle. Three lines are then drawn in the circle as in illustration A. Fold as in illustration B.

Now ask them to write in the three spaces three characteristics of themselves – positives and negatives. Gently push for quick responses – not long drawn out boring pauses.

The paper is then swopped with the partner, who completes the other side without looking at the first side. The partner is briefed to write three words describing the other person's characteristics – same brief.

On completion, discuss in twos or as a small group. Compare own view with partner's view of self. As with most games, the leader's input is very important.

NOTES

Be sensitive, especially if vulnerable people are present. A minority of young people can be hard and use this game to be spiteful. Encourage affirmation – see other games on this.

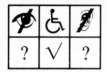

Envelope

OBJECTIVE

To facilitate self-awareness and an experience of affirmation using the Bible.

NUMBERS

All present large group or similar.

EQUIPMENT

Psalm 139 (a modern version is better). A small envelope and a pen or pencil for each person.

DETAILS

Introduce the game by asking all present to write on the outside of the envelope they have been given. Stress that the envelope is now their property and it will not be handed back in or seen by anyone else. It is totally confidential.

Phase One
Ask participants to write on the outside of the envelope their personal characteristics which are known to others. Strengths and weaknesses, positives, negatives. The *public* facts about themselves. Stress it's confidential.

Phase Two
Ask them to write inside the envelopes their personal characteristics which are not known to others. Strengths, weaknesses, positives and negatives. Stress confidentiality. Encourage them to take risks by being honest.

Phase three
They all seal their envelope and hold it tightly to their chests.

Phase four
The participants are asked to close their eyes, listen and absorb the Bible reading. The group worker then reads out the whole, or part, of Psalm 139, putting much emphasis on the affirming, valuing verses.

Phase five
No further activity is really necessary. But if you feel it needs a further interaction or contribution, either use note 2 below, or just get the group members to share their feelings. Don't overkill by trying to squeeze too much out of a very personal experience.

NOTES

1. Prepare the Bible reading.
2. Phase four can be introduced or ended by a short comment from the group worker, such as: "This Bible passage shows God's total unconditional love. His valuing of us, his acceptance of us, knowing – as God does – all our thoughts and activities." Keep it very brief.

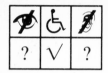

Romford YMCA

(Use the name of your own club, hall, church)

OBJECTIVE

Co-operation in groups

NUMBERS

All present in groups of 6 to 10.

EQUIPMENT

Loads – see separate list

DETAILS

Split everyone present into groups of 6 to 10 (no fewer than 6). Introduce the game by saying it is a group exercise in creativity. Each group is issued with the equipment and a brief. Either read out the brief or, better still, provide it on paper for each group.

When the "Go" is given the group will have 20 minutes to design and build a symbolic castle which will visually demonstrate your ideal YMCA (Replace YMCA with a relevant building to which your group identifies, e.g. community centre, village hall, youth club, Scout hut, church). All the equipment provided must be used.

Once they begin the group worker plays the role of a silent observer without giving any additional advice, information or assistance. (If there are several groups, it may be useful to have an experienced group person/observer per group.)

When just five minutes are left, announce each minute to build up the pressure.

EQUIPMENT FOR EACH GROUP

Large crisp box or similar
Sellotape – small roll
String – small ball
2 sheets of A3 size paper
5 or 6 felt-tip pens

10 paperclips
10 colour magazines – Sunday
    newspaper type
3 (or more) pairs of scissors
A table

End the game promptly. Do it firmly but with some care and sensitivity.

Ask participants to stand still and think how they feel. (Silence can re-emphasise feelings, and an outbreak of laughter or conversation will take away the positive process of the game.)

Then go around asking all participants to say in one word how they feel.

Use these feelings to illustrate that a silly game with cardboard can create real feelings of pleasure, frustration, even anger (use their words). Once you have used these feelings well, turn to next phase.

Next Phase is when more than one group has participated. Get all present to move around to each "Castle" to have the group describe the thinking and meaning behind the structure. This is interesting – seeing the creativity of people, how they display their beliefs and values.

If appropriate, get people into their small task groups again to discuss the roles played during the building process, with the help of the observer. Considerable learning can take place through this process.

Empathy – High Low

OBJECTIVE

A process of interactions which raises awareness of one's own feelings and those of others. To understand, empathise and therefore be more equipped to be sensitive in relationships and interventions.

EQUIPMENT

None

NUMBERS

Important.
Essentially and definitely one small group – not more than 8 – ideally 6 to 8. AND one sensitive and experienced group worker.

DETAILS

Process the group through an ice breaking sequence, for example:
1. Vote with feet (p. 45)
2. Blob Tree etc. (p. 98)
3. Quickies p. 179 to 183
Use Loads of affirmation – acknowledging and valuing their co-operation and commitment to interact. Process the group into an attitude of co-operation which *excludes* humour, unsolicited comments and other distractions. This needs a commitment to "going deep". Open up the group to share their own feelings, for example Blob Tree page 98 or other Blob pics. Emphasis needs to be on feelings not position, or what they THINK: feelings not thoughts.
Taking the Blob Tree as an example here, the next step is to

ask the group members to pluck from their minds a young person they know whom they are concerned about.

1. Firstly share a description of that person – in twos or threes.
2. Then return to Blob Tree, and group members are asked to do this game on behalf of that young person. Again the emphasis is on feelings. It is best done in twos or threes. So the process re that young person has been (i) a description of him or her and a description of what is of concern about that young person. (ii) Blob Tree sharing game, describing the feelings of the young person.

By now the participants will be more aware and in touch with that young person emotionally.

Awareness is now raised and engaged.

3. Ask the group to stand. Re-emphasise the need for silence, the absence of giggling, quips, unsolicited comments, etc. Then go on to ask them to empathise with the individual's feelings in the context of their group, and display/demonstrate that person's feelings by the position of their own body, i.e. standing, stretching high for positive – flat on the floor for extreme negative, or somewhere in between. The group now begin to crouch, bend, lean, lie – whatever their interpretation may be of that person they know.
4. Verbalise that you are allowing a little time of silence so that they can, in that still position, feel with depth. Then ask them, each in turn, to complete this sentence "I feel . . . ".
   the room is then filled with slowly delivered feeling statements from the mouths of youth workers, but in wonderful empathy with a person they want to love and desire to love and care for.
5. That's it. Group members can then regain their seats and become themselves again. The next phase is allowing and encouraging them to express how they feel. Usually there is a wonderfully raised awareness of the kids they work with. Let them work it out – don't leave them with feelings either high or extreme. Feelings games like this need a de-roling phase. See page 155.

NOTES

What can go wrong:

1. Lack of seriousness and commitment.
2. Group leader's lack of sensitivity, and pacing the game incorrectly.
3. Insufficient climate of trust in the group.
4. Hostility from group to the leader due to their experience of extreme feelings which make them feel uncomfortable.

Quickies

Quickies – Quickly put. But no less valuable or powerful

Good Group Games

Quickies can last long or be short, but are very enjoyable – and useful as a developing process for all of us humans.

1. Write a description of your perfect day. List 10 activities you enjoy most. Reveal your deepest needs and longings. Be honest!
2. Everyone invents a Red Indian name for him or herself. Then they "do" the name with actions. Let the mind go wild.
3. Everyone shares three things, from the time when they were about seven years old:
   i) The way their home was heated – describe home and the system of heating.
   ii) The person who was the warmest in their lives at that age.
   iii) Warmth of feeling, or otherwise, towards God at that age. If they have no memory of God then, relate the first-ever warm experience of God.
4. Squiggle on paper one line which describes your life and feelings at this very moment. Everyone explains their own squiggly line.
5. Draw around a person as they lie on the floor, on paper. Then everyone cuts out of colour magazines pictures that describe or illustrate the positives of that person, sticking them onto the body shape. After it's all finished, everyone talks about their own contributions.
6. Everyone writes on a sheet of paper 6 things which they have in their pocket/handbag at the moment. Mix the sheets up and pick one each. Then read them out one by one, and everyone else has to guess who wrote which list.
7. Everyone writes a "for sale" advert for themselves, presuming it would have to be concise and placed in the local paper.

8. Everyone takes a piece of paper and draws a vertical line on each end of it, with a central horizontal line joining them. The left line is birth, the one on the right is now. Draw one more line up and down showing a peak and trough describing the age when they had highs and lows. Use drawings to talk/share.

9. Everyone talks about their name in turn, saying what they THINK and FEEL about all its parts. Leader starts the process by being very open and revealing.

10. Everyone writes 1,2,3, on paper with the following favourites: (1) place in the home, (2) time of the day, (3) TV/Radio Programme. Mix them up and pick one each. Then guess who wrote what, as in (6) above.

11. Everyone closes eyes and, following two minutes' silence and thinking time, each draw a plan of their childhood dinner table – the people, the plates, etc., from an early meal memory. Share.

12. Fire Drill – everyone quickly lists on paper which things they would rescue from a house fire at home (presuming humans and animals are safe). Mix and pick, or just talk about it.

13. Everyone describes themselves on paper, leaving out their job/school/college, relationships, and any activities they do. Mix and pick as (6) above.

14. Everyone icebreaks by pinning a paper on their chests with the following already written: (i) Name they wish to be known by (centre), (ii) Favourite place in the world (top left), (iii) Person of influence on their life (top right), (iv) Strongest feature in personality (bottom left), (v) Place of birth (bottom right). Everyone mixes, talking about each other's chest!

15. Circle Question. Go around the group responding to these questions in turn. What is:
    i) The best news I have read recently
    ii) The most satisfying event during the last week
    iii) The most recent news which has caused me concern
    iv) The most exciting thing in my life at the moment

16. Everyone stands in a circle and gently throws a ball or something similar to another in the group saying for example, (i) "My name is Jenny and I like U2" (ii) "My name is Winston and I like Mars Bars".

17. Everyone, in groups of 10–15, stands in two lines facing one another, and they become a car wash. Each decides which part of a car wash they want to be. One person goes through the car wash at a time, to receive the strokes "rubbing" and "patting".

End Games

Pins on Backs

OBJECTIVE

To enable a group to affirm each other, offering each other valuable comments in a structured and developmental manner

NUMBERS

All present

EQUIPMENT

Supply of straight (dressmaker's) pins
Supply of A4 sheets of paper
Felt-tip pens (domestic type – small tips)

SITUATION

1. Good as an ending activity following a conference, course, houseparty, etc.
2. Good for mid-training course experience with view to more intense work/training.
3. Not suitable for icebreaker unless all group members present know each other.

DETAILS

See Section Two: Bits and Pieces Affirmation Sheet p. 149.

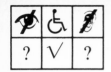

Zig-Zag

OBJECTIVE

Development of individuals and the life of a group

NUMBERS

Best with small groups of 6 to 10, who know each other at least a little

EQUIPMENT

A pen or pencil for each person
A long slim piece of paper for each person (cut A4 sheets down the centre lengthways)

DETAILS

With the group sitting in a circle, hand out the paper and pens and ask each person to write his or her name at the top. They all pass their papers to the left.

Each person now writes one word or one sentence in the bottom half-inch of the paper, stating something they value and appreciate about the person named.

It is then folded over (to hide the comment) before passing on to the next person. The paper circulates the group, with comments being added and folded over. (Leader note: Demonstrate to make it very simple for participants.)

The outcome is a completed list of comments, which is now returned to its owner.

For best results – forbid members to read any comments until all the papers return to their owners. Then ask them to read in silence – no noise or comments. The silence helps to deliver the impact needed.

The discussion which follows needs to be well led to promote personal development, with individual and whole group dynamic in mind.

NOTES

Other suggestions for individual comments:
a One animal which reminds you of this person's personality.
b One positive characteristic about this person.
c A Disney cartoon character which best describes this person's personality.
d One weakness which you see in this person.

Only use d in the context of other activities which build positively on what is said – it can be destructive if not used with sensitivity and very skilled leadership.

It can be useful in a well established group, growing together in the middle of a weekend training event, with time to talk through inevitable hurts – and to end with a building-up exercise.

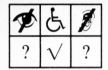

Knitty Wool Pattern

OBJECTIVE

To end a training course or group meeting, or weekend, in a positive manner.

NUMBERS

Everyone present in groups of 10

EQUIPMENT

One ball of wool for each group
One pair of scissors for each group

DETAILS

Groups sit in a circle facing each other.
One member holds the ball of wool and talks about him/herself. Things to say: what I like about me, a talent of mine. That person keeps hold of the wool, and passes the ball to any other member of the group, who also talks, keeps hold of the wool and passes on the ball.
At the end, ask everyone who is born between January and July to drop the wool, and ask the others to take up the slack wool. They will find the pattern is ruined when some are not involved. The rest of the group has fallen apart, because some people have just dropped out! This happens in real life.
Get them all to hold on to the wool again and pass a pair of scissors to each group.
The END of the meeting is when the wool is cut in the centre of the circle.

Designing Your Own Growth Game

Any reasonably experienced leader can design games. You may feel it isn't possible. It just needs sitting down and thinking about the needs of the group and being resourceful.

If you are willing to have a go, here is some structure to work from.

1. Decide which group you would like to design a game for.
2. Decide on your aim, the result you want to achieve – ideally having consulted and received some input from the group in question – or the group leader.
3. Consider all these factors:

   The setting – where the game will be played
   Participants – who will be there
   General objectives – yours, theirs (both leaders and "the people")

   Capabilities of the participants – their willingness, anxieties, sex mix, any physical or mental disabilities, etc., and trust.
   Constraints – Rules, roles and resources that will effect your activities.
4. Decide if you want to influence:

   a Life skills – skills/response capabilities, etc., e.g. a flight simulator will develop skills in flying, an "almost real" game will deliver skills.
   b Inside the person – their feelings. Raising people's awareness can help equip them for future life – coping themselves, and with increased skills to help in other people's lives.

5. Choose style of Game.

Styles	Board Game	Mix and pick
	Card Game	
	in tray.	

TYPES OF GAMES

Board Game   Monopoly, Trivial Pursuits

Card Game   Snap, I'm all right Jack

In Tray   Handout Sheet type. TASK given to group members

Mix and pick Individuals input, or worker-led, resulting in a random distribution of tasks or questions etc. see p. 117

Pen and Paper Members given tasks to write, draw, etc.

Role Play   Set up an 'experience' for analysis

6. Play the game in your head and on paper. Give special attention to start and finish.

7. Prepare, make equipment, write handouts, monopoly cards etc. Always use issues and topics relevant to the target group.

8. Go for it – using all sensitivity and purpose.

The Rolling Magazine Video

*These are also in *Games Without Frontiers*, Pip Wilson, 1988

Introduction to the Video of the Magazine of the Book

There is also a video which lines up with this book – produced partly by professionals and partly by amateurs. It is published by Greenbelt (see appendix for address). It shows my head talking away about Rolling Magazine interaction games and features a number of games "in action".

If you can put up with seeing my head framed in your television set, you could pick up from it lots of ideas and thoughts and reflections about Rolling Magazine style events. Obviously a visual on TV has more impact than words in a book – but even the visual impact is not as good as the real thing when you play the games.

Games are meant to be experienced. Experiences are meant to be experienced. Interactive exercises can only really happen when there's a real interaction.

Looking at the games being played on video when you are not in the context can obviously seem strange. That's why I put such a special emphasis on building atmosphere, building a climate of trust, building a rock 'n' roll climate to help young people feel at ease and therefore be willing to put themselves at risk and therefore step outside their comfort boundaries into areas of growth and development. The games shown on the video and described in this section are all about facilitating young people, or in fact any group of people, to develop their potential in body, mind and spirit.

This chapter in the book lists every game and every technique which is talked about on the video in the order it appears there. It is not particularly recommended that you play them in that order – in fact, it is best not to! One of the principles of the Rolling Magazine is that there isn't a programme but there *is* a repertoire, and items of programme are slotted in at the most appropriate moment.

Dive into the whole book – and my other *Games Without Frontiers*. You have hundreds of games to choose from. Go go.

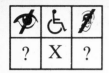

| ? | X | ? |

Horse Race

OBJECTIVE

Good fun

NUMBERS

2 couples, or more

EQUIPMENT

2 eggs
2 blindfolds

DETAILS

Boys become the horse and the girls jump on their backs. Give instructions about the obstacle course.
Say you will count down 5 4 3 2 1 GO.
Just before Go, produce boys' blindfolds – the girls have to give directions to the blind horse.
Say 5 4 3 2 1 STOP!
You have just remembered that the girls have to hold an egg between their teeth.
5 4 3 2 1 GO!

SPECIAL NOTES

Run around marquee poles or some other hurdles.
Ask the audience to stay where they are and *not* move out of their way.
A good audience game – they love it when the egg breaks down the boy's neck!

🐢	♿	🏃
?	X	?

Knee Sit

OBJECTIVE

Good fun, total participation, icebreaker

NUMBERS

Everybody (minimum 8–10)

EQUIPMENT

None

DETAILS

Get everyone into groups of approximately 10. Form into circles with the same shoulder facing into the centre and tightly packed close to one another.

On the word "Go", the group should slowly sit down on the knees of the person behind them.

When successful the next phase is to walk or shuffle around with hands in the air to the beat of music.

SPECIAL NOTES

The circle must be "round" and the more tightly packed the better. Expect heaps of people.
Try two groups together! Then try a big one, with *everyone* in one circle.

Group Hug

OBJECTIVE

Icebreaker, participation, cohesiveness builder

NUMBERS

Everybody

EQUIPMENT

None

DETAILS

Get all present into circles of approximately 10 people, standing shoulder to shoulder. Get everyone to put their arms over each other's shoulders in a linked circle. Count down and on "Go" everyone is invited to give the group a big group hug.

Ask them to share how it feels, then re-play.

Join more groups together, if appropriate, and end with all those present having a big group hug.

NOTES

If they are familiar with "Get Knotted" (game 10 in *Games Without Frontiers*), get them in circles and pretend you are about to replay that. Then turn it into a Group Hug instead.

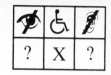

Grape Tread

OBJECTIVE

Messy-fun stunt

NUMBERS

3 volunteers

EQUIPMENT

3 bunches of grapes
3 large plastic bowls (washing-up bowls)
3 sieves and jugs
3 large clear plastic cups

DETAILS

Introduce this as a game needing strength and energy.
The volunteers face the audience, roll up their trousers and remove their foot gear.
They are then instructed to tread the grapes, during the playing of a pop record, and make wine.
At the end, the mixture is sieved and each one measured.
The loser or, better, all three have to drink the wine.

SPECIAL NOTES

Wonderful game for the audience!
A good enthusiastic crowd will encourage this game to a good conclusion.
It is very important that *volunteers* are recruited.

Baked-Bean Trifle

OBJECTIVE

Big time fun

NUMBERS

3 couples

EQUIPMENT

3 very large clear funnels
3 12″ lengths of clear hose to fit on end of funnels
3 clear plastic jugs
Cleaning up materials
Baked-Bean Trifle (see Notes)

DETAILS

Make sure you get real volunteers for this one.
It needs a big build-up; best used at the end of games session.
The boy stands on a chair behind his mate who holds the lip of the funnel between her teeth.
Tuck end of hose down the front of her upper garment.
With much ceremony hand the Baked-Bean Trifle to the boys.
Questions are then asked to the girls and when the answer is wrong or the word "pass" is used the Trifle is demonstratively poured into the funnel.
The audience love it.

NOTES

You could do a preliminary round using water! It's good to do a round of very simple easy-to-answer questions, followed by impossible-to-answer questions.

Ingredients for Baked-Bean Trifle
1 large family sized tin baked beans
1 packet instant custard
1 packet Dream Topping (made up with water)
1 cherry!
Doing a swap at the last moment adds to the fun.

?	?	?

Porridge

OBJECTIVE

Large group stunt for fun

NUMBERS

3 or 4 couples

EQUIPMENT

Per couple:
Large clear plastic funnel
Clear plastic tube 12″ long × 1½″ bore
Jug of porridge
List of questions – see below

DETAILS

Have 3 jugs of cold porridge standing ready.
Get the volunteers, ideally boy and girlfriends, in couples.
Boys (or girls) grip the lip of funnel in mouth.
The tube is fixed to the funnel with other end of tube tucked into the boys' trousers.
Questions are asked and if participants get it wrong, or say "pass", their partner gives them the porridge.

See Appendix for suggested questions for participants.

Instant Buzz Questions

OBJECTIVE

To open up the sharing of self to another – increasing in detail in a non-threatening style

NUMBERS

All present

EQUIPMENT

None

DETAILS

Ask participants to turn to the person next to them, in twos or threes, and answer the following instant questions. The idea is to ask quick instant-reaction questions, occasionally asking the question "Why?" E.g. Who would you chose to be – the Prime Minister of his bodyguard? Other examples of choices:

Would rather have or be:

Indian meal	or	Chinese meal
Nike trainers	or	Un-named shoes from local market
Sun newspaper	or	Guardian
Winter	or	Summer
C.D.	or	Walkman
Terry Wogan	or	Simon Mayo
Humpty Dumpty	or	King's (wo)man
Taker	or	Giver
Leader	or	Follower
Thinker	or	Doer
Listener	or	Talker

Colour of

OBJECTIVE

Fun way to help participants think and share their view of themselves, of someone they admire and of God

NUMBERS

All present

EQUIPMENT

None

DETAILS

In the midst of other activities ask all participants to turn to the person next to them and in twos or threes answer the following questions:

1. What colour are you? (Not skin colour – all questions relate to the colour which describes your personality and character.)
2. Who would you like to be stuck in a lift with? What colour is that person?
3. What colour is God?

If appropriate share answers with larger group. All these answers are opinions – not right or wrong. Encourage participants to listen without arguing or differing. Affirm all answers, value all humans.

✏	♿	✏
√	√	?

Last Telephone Call

OBJECTIVE

Enable participants to think of, and share in a non-threatening way, who they value in life, and emphasise their (often) lack of expression of love to those they love.

NUMBERS

All present

EQUIPMENT

None

DETAILS

Ask all participants to turn to the person alongside them and share in twos and threes:

1. Which person would they telephone if they knew they were to die in the next two minutes?
2. Next step: ask them to share what they would say.
3. Next step: ask them to share with their partners when was the last time they said to the person they named, "I love you".

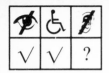

Level 5

OBJECTIVE

To demonstrate by experience how communication can be much more meaningful than people's "normal" interaction. To lead people gently into deeper levels and have a positive individual and group outcome in development terms.

NUMBERS

All present

EQUIPMENT

None

DETAILS

Take a look first at the discussion on Level 5 and the graphic on page 26.
In the midst of other group activities, having established a climate of trust and participation, share the Level 5 model. Then ask participants to share with the person next to them, in twos or threes, answers to the following questions.
These are samples – please use your own as appropriate.

NOTES

Be sensitive with people. Observe everyone and take note of anyone who shows distress. Sometimes sharing feelings can disturb a person and there is need for counselling (informal/formal, first aid, professional).

EXERCISE/GAME	FOLLOW-UP – LEADER GUIDANCE-INPUT
Level 1 Cliché Communication. *Question*: Talk about the weather for two minutes.	Point out to the group how really boring it is to talk about the weather when you have established a relationship.
Level 2 Communication of **Fact**. *Question*: Talk about the last TV programme you saw, keeping to the facts of what you saw and heard.	Observe and relate to those present how (almost as boring) it is to stick to the task. Receive confessions from those who didn't follow the task and laugh together about it.
Level 3 Communication of **Opinions**. *Question*: Ask those present to talk about some topical issue, e.g. AIDS, war, murder, political incidents, etc.	Observe and relate to those present how much more interesting it is to give something of yourself to another, and to hear opinions. Acknowledge that it often relates only to the head – not the heart.
Level 4 Communication of **Feelings** *Question*: Ask just one participant to share, in the context of the small groups of twos/threes, not all having a go! Ask them to share the most important concern in their life at the moment. Stress the confidentiality of it. Ask that it be open, honest, risk-taking, and that it be kept confidential between talker and listener(s) only.	Observe and relate to those present by asking questions. 1. How do they feel. Allow individuals to express their feelings. Go public if appropriate or ask them to share in their small groups. 2. Ask them to share the satisfaction or otherwise. Affirm those who offer sensitive contributions. Have the whole group present hear and receive the feedback – if at all possible, let the whole group benefit from the interactions experienced in the small groups.
Level 5 Total Openness in Communication. No questions.	Express how Level 5 is an extension of Level 4 – feelings and intimate sharing which can only be developed in the context of a trusting relationship.

BHP Affirmation

OBJECTIVE

Group building, giving encouragement in all too often negative world. BHP = Beautiful Human Person.

NUMBERS

About 6 to 10

EQUIPMENT

None

DETAILS

Everyone gets into groups of 6 to 10, and they form a circle.
Everyone puts arms around each other's shoulders in group hug formation.
Ask everyone to tell the person on their right one thing that they like about that person. Affirmation then goes round the circle.

SPECIAL NOTES

Encourage participants to try to do this without laughing and being too embarrassed.
We are not experienced enough at giving and receiving affirmation.
It is most beneficial if the game is played with real openness and honesty.

Group Massage

OBJECTIVE

An activity which gives all participants the opportunity to receive and give physical affirmation in a non-threatening manner (and it's nice!)

NUMBERS

All present in groups of 6 to 15

EQUIPMENT

None

DETAILS

Ask everyone present to stand in circles of about 10 people. (This can also be played with everyone present in one circle.) Everyone is asked to turn their left shoulder into the centre, and raise their left hand, then the right hand, and bring them in turn down gently onto the shoulders of the person in front of them.

On "Go", or after a group countdown from 10, the whole group is asked to massage the other person's shoulders gently and affirmingly. (A second phase can be turning around and massaging a different person.) Don't let it drag on too long.

Marshmallow Drop

OBJECTIVE

A stunt with good fun

NUMBERS

3 couples are best

EQUIPMENT

3 packets of jelly babies, marshmallows or similar
3 plastic water cups
3 cups of chocolate dip or sauce
3 paper towels

DETAILS

The girls stand on chairs above the heads of the boys, who are holding cups in their mouths while lying on backs.
On the word "Go" the girls dip a jelly baby in chocolate and drop the sweet into the cup. (It often misses!) When all "babies" are dropped the girls are encouraged to pour the remaining chocolate at the same target.

SPECIAL NOTES

It is a messy game but the better for it.
Only use towels if the dress warrants it!
Give a prize to the winner – the messiest!!
Variation: drop the jelly babies into the boys' mouths instead of in the cups, and they have to eat one before the next is dropped.

| ? | X | ? |

Making Love

OBJECTIVE

Group fun with cohesiveness-building benefits

NUMBERS

Everybody (minimum 25)

EQUIPMENT

None

DETAILS

Get everyone into groups of 10 or so in a line and holding hands.

Count how many groups and decide on a word with that number of letters.

On the word "Go" the groups have to form a letter each that spells the word.

For example, "Greenbelt" will need nine groups, with one group forming each letter.

Allow the group to decide how to do it, and watch the fun.

For the first go, it's fun to ask them to "make love" – L-O-V-E (of course).

SPECIAL NOTES

This game encourages large group co-operation, and small group co-operation.

Repeat with other words but don't overdo it!

Alternative: shout out a number (say 6) and *each* group has to decide on a word with six letters in it and spell it, using their bodies.

This is more competitive, the other game is more co-operative.

Appendix

List of Crazy Questions and Stunts

Objective

Use these to "knockout" fun competitors during fun games
The questions and answers that follow:

1. Some can only be answered "PASS"
2. Others are "difficult" – the nearest answer to the correct one
   – WINS
   – the biggest miss of the mark – LOSES
3. *Others are impossible*
4. *Others totally imbalanced* – crazy – just crazy

Sample List of Crazy Questions

QUESTION *Impossible to WIN*	ANSWER
1. A bird in the hand . . .?	Does it on your wrist
2. Two rugby players running side by side throwing the ball to each other is called a . . .	Pass
3. The divide between two mountains is called a valley sometimes and is also called a . . .	Pass
4. A girl chasing a boy with lips puckered is making a . . .	Pass
5. A bus ticket for an extended period is accompanied by a bus . . .	Pass
6. Going abroad you need a . . .? port.	Pass
7. How many spots on a leopard?	You are wrong
8. How many full stops in a bottle of ink?	You are wrong
9. What is the name of Pip's tortoise?	You are wrong (He hasn't got one!)
10. Now go crazy – make up your own!	

Kissing Questions with Answers

1. What is the longest ever screen kiss?
   ans: 185 seconds

2. What is the longest ever underwater kiss?
   ans: 2 min 18 seconds

3. A long lingering kiss exercises 29 facial muscles true/false
   ans: true

4. What's the record for the longest kiss ever?
   ans: 17 days 10½ hours

5. The first ever screen kiss was filmed in either 1920, 1830, 1896
   ans: 1896

6. In London 59% of people kiss on the lips each day, and in Scotland only 38% true/false
   ans: true

7. Kissing cuts tooth decay? true/false
   ans: true

8. Each kiss burns up more than 3 calories? true/false
   ans: true

9. Who was the roughest kisser in hollywood? Joan Collins, Timothy Dalton, Marlene Dietrich
   ans: Marlene Dietrich

10. How many types of bacteria are exchanged when 2 people kiss?
    ans: 250

11. An anthropologist claims that only 37% of women keep their eyes closed when kissing but 97% of men true/false
    ans: false 97% women 37% men

12. Kissing reduces your life span by 3 minutes per kiss?
    ans: true

List of Crazy Stunts

1. Throw your trousers to the other side of the room – whilst still wearing them

2. Impersonate – Batman and Robin conversation
   Mrs Thatcher
   John Major
   Favourite Soap Star
   Me
   Laurel and Hardy Conversation

3. Sing a Beatles song

4. Exchange three items of clothing with your partner

Using Videos in Groups

1. Long films kill a group! They murder a group dynamic unless your objective is just a lazy relaxing evening.
   Short 10–15 minute videos, with impact, can set a group alight
   See it first. Edit good bits. Show the best ones!
   Show it.
   Get re-action – from them – leader comes last
   Questions can help growth
   Sermons – leave them in church

2. If you have a programme of videos over a few weeks – vary them. See issues ideas enclosed. Mix obvious Christian stuff with current issues. Tape off TV – but keep it stinking short – 5–7 minutes will do – just remember how boring some 3-minute songs are on TV pop shows.

Pip's Video Recommendations

There are others but . . . yuk!

1. *Christian Impact*	*Source (See Addresses)*
Music Box	1236
Humpty	1236
Selfish Giant	1236
Cross & The Switchblade	1243
Tanglewood Secrets	126
Treasures in the Snow	123
The Hiding Place	1236
Corrie	1236
Enry	6
No.1 Plus Others	7 shops
Dead Poets Society	shops
Ben Hur	6
The Velveteen Rabbit	10
The Mission	shops
The Parable	XYZ

2. *Music*	
Bruce Cockburn in Concert	8
U2 Rattle & Hum	shops
Mike Yaconelli	8
Steve Taylor	1243
Martyn Joseph in Concert	8

3. *Tools/Ideas*	
Rolling Magazine Video	8
Skill Training – Violence	4
Sexual Abuse	4
Sexual Abuse talking to	4
kids	4
Difficult Incidents	
Management Training (expensive)	5

Make your own from TV – start your Library NOW. Shoot your own – borrow a video camera (or loan from local shop) and roll your film. ASK for free dud tapes from your record shop and tape over them.

SOURCES

1. Word Videos, 9 Holdom Avenue, Milton Keynes, MK1 1QU.
2. Bagster Video, 76 High Street, Alton, Hants. GU34 1EN.
3. International Films, 235 Shaftesbury Ave, London WC2H 8EL.
4. Audio Visual Services, Leeds University, Leeds LS2 9JT.
5. Gower TFI Ltd, Croft Road, Aldershot, Hants. GU11 3HR.
6. Trinity Video, 76 High Street, Alton, Hants. GU34 1EN.
7. Scripture Union 9–11 Clothier Street, Bristol.
8. Greenbelt, The Greenhouse, Hillmarton Road, London N7 9JE.
9. Shelter Bunty Video, 10a The Pavement, Clapham Common SW4 0HY.
10. CTS, 38–40 Eccleston Square, London SW1V 1PD.
11. Health Education Council, 78 New Oxford St., London W1A 1AH.
12. League Against Cruel Sports, 83–87 Union St., London SE1 1SG.
13. YMCA National Council, 640 Forest Road, London E17 3DZ.
14. Animal Rights, 2 Lavant St, Petersfield, Hants. GU32 3EW.
15. F.P.A. 27–35 Mortimer Street, London W1N 7RJ.
16. Greenpeace, 36 Graham Street, London N1 8LL.

XYZ, The Parable which is an old "NO WORDS" film about a Clown/Jesus. Let me know if you get it? I would love a copy!

Games Questionnaire for Preparation Event

Need to lead a games session?
- intend to run a Rolling Magazine in an unknown venue/context?

PREPARATION SHEET NOTES

Ask these questions to yourself and _____

(Name of Key Contact)

Type of Event

Date _____

Day _____

Arrival Time _____

Start Time _____

Finish Time _____

Size of Hall (Venue) _____

Ceiling High/Low _____

Stage

    Fixed _____

    Portable _____

    Height _____

    Width _____

    Depth _____

Power points & location _____

Lighting available/fixed _____

Sound System available/fixed _____

Catering Facilities for workers/punters _____

The Targeted Humans

Ages _____

Numbers _____

Male _____

Female _____

Social Background _____

Normal Social Interests _____

One Group _____

Cohesive _____

Individuals of Note _____

Christian Commitment _____

Local Tension _____

Local Issues/Concerns _____

Recent Programme _____

Attitude to Messy Games _____

Attitude to Christian Games _____

Expectations of Participants _____

Expectation of Organisers _____

Re-Action Sheet

Good management of anything follows this process
1. Evaluate
2. Make Policy
3. Assign Roles
4. Monitor Performance

This is a suggested, well tested, handout to help the group leader. YOU. It is a means of EVALUATING your activity/event/game/Rolling Magazine

Facilitation Feedback? use The Re-action Sheet!
Photocopy this and use for as many sessions as you can. It's feedback, it's also good therapy.

RE-ACTION SHEET   NAME _____

CIRCLE ONE

1. *How helpful was the session?*

   *   *   *   *   *   *   *   *

   very poor medi– fair good very excel–   best
   poor   ocre   good ent   ever

---

2. *To what extent did it deal with your real interests/needs?*

   *   *   *   *   *   *

   not at all   a bit   some   very much   right on

---

3. *What was the main strength?*

   _____

   _____

   _____

---

4. *What was the main weakness?*

   _____

   _____

   _____

Note to Leader. Distribute This

A sheet to give out *before* the event! Photocopy the Blob Balloons on reverse side
Well what do you expect?

OBJECTIVE

This gives everyone an opportunity to tune into their expectations. We all have them!

Use this with the Blob Balloons Handout

EXPECTATION SHEET

INSTRUCTIONS

Place in each BLOB Balloon an answer to any or all of these questions:

1. What do I expect to happen first?
2. What do I expect to happen next?
3. What do I expect from the leader?
4. What did I expect to do?
5. How am I expected to respond?
6. What do I expect from others?
7. I have come here today because ....
8. I expect to give ....
9. I expect to receive ....
10. I expect to feel ....
11. I am feeling at this moment ....

Note the Blob Balloons handout can be used for many re-action type activities – it's better than boring old plain paper.